The Mill in
the Schwaig

The Mill in
the Schwaig

*A story of God's faithfulness and
grace over many years in the lives of
Lilian and Robert Schunneman*

ISOBEL VALE

Scripture quotations are taken from The Holy Bible,
New International Version (Anglicised edition)
Copyright © 1979, 1984, 2011 by Biblica

All information is correct at the time of going to press.
Any inaccuracies will be corrected in any future edition.

Matador
9 Priory Business Park,
Wistow Road, Kibworth Beauchamp,
Leicestershire. LE8 0RX
Tel: 0116 279 2299
Email: books@troubador.co.uk
Web: www.troubador.co.uk/matador
Twitter: @matadorbooks

ISBN 978 1800463 462

British Library Cataloguing in Publication Data.
A catalogue record for this book is available from the British Library.

Printed and bound by CPI Group (UK) Ltd, Croydon, CR0 4YY
Typeset in 11pt Minion Pro by Troubador Publishing Ltd, Leicester, UK

Matador is an imprint of Troubador Publishing Ltd

'Called to serve God through a ministry which was committed to children.' Rob and Lil Schunneman share inspiring, challenging experiences of the faithfulness of the God whom they trusted, in all the changing scenes of their life at 'The Mill' in Großgmain, Austria. It is a poignant and powerful story of two people; whose mission focus began by joining others in caring for orphans and physically building them a home. This house, the Schwaigmühle, provided a loving family environment and over the years became a strategic centre for children, young people and many others who enjoyed Bible teaching and fellowship, with many discovering the Christian faith for themselves.'

David Cook, Chairman,
Child Evangelism Fellowship of Britain

Contents

Introduction

This book tells the story of Robert and Lilian Schunneman. Although originally from America and England respectively, they lived and worked as missionaries in the Salzburg region of Austria for many years.

The material for this book has been drawn from notes and events relating to their lives and family, alongside information from English and American contacts. Most importantly however, the details come from the Schunnemans themselves, mostly through conversations over many years. Their actual words are retained as far as possible. I may be the official author, but in essence, they are the real authors of this book as they speak through the narrative. I think they would also want to say that God is the true author. He had a plan for their lives, and they followed.

Lilian begins their story in the Preface, after which we trace their lives, firstly as individuals, then together, and witness the faithfulness of God at every stage.

Isobel Vale
Oxford, England
Summer 2020

Preface

Even to your old age... I will carry you.

Isaiah 46 v 4

One hundred and eighty years, that was our combined age, when Rob and I celebrated our ninetieth birthdays, in our church in Graz, with our family and friends on 26 October 2019. Our daughter, Elizabeth, masterminded the whole project and together with Isobel Vale, a long-time friend from England, plans were made. I wasn't sure if I wanted to be the centre of attention, nor was I sure that Rob would want to celebrate, as his health was worsening. However, together, we decided it would be good to celebrate now and not wait until our funerals when family and friends would gather together.

We agreed on a celebration, but I had some particular requests; it must be a fun party with people dressing up, games and activities. A theme was hatched – an 'English/ American tea party'. Practical preparations had been going on for several days before, with an extensive exhibition of our lives being created around the room, music being practised, English and American cakes being baked and tables beautifully set. Red and white flowers adorned the tables with stars and stripes serviettes and special birthday confetti added to our theme.

And so, to the actual day of the tea party. Guests had been invited to dress 'to fit with the theme', and many did. Some took on an American style: cowboys/cowgirls, Indians, sheriffs and one grandson dressed in Rob's navy officer uniform, wonderfully preserved over many years. Others took on an English theme, dressing for a posh afternoon tea with hair fascinators and pretty dresses or elegant suits with bowler hats, rather like Charlie Chaplin. Rob wore his favourite American tie.

Rob and I became 'King and Queen' for the afternoon and this was most fitting, for as everyone who knows me is aware, I am a great enthusiast of the English Queen, Elizabeth II. I was honoured to be Queen and have Rob at my side as King. Thanks to English friends, we wore some splendid gold jewelled crowns and our chairs became 'thrones', covered with the relevant flag. We had regal capes draped over our shoulders.

The huge exhibition, meticulously set up by Elizabeth, showed our lives from birth to the present day. I could hardly believe all the objects and artefacts which had not only survived a fire at The Mill but had also endured such long journeys from America to England to Ireland, from Ireland to Salzburg and eventually to Stainz. So much to see and admire: a model train set, brought back for The Mill children in the 1960s, letter scales still in use today, photo albums, a globe, children's books, a cookbook which had belonged to Rob's mother, postcards and a letter written to Rob's grandmother when he was twelve. These were just a few of the items on display, the rest, too numerous to list. Here we were, with our family and friends, across several generations, looking back on our lives, so grateful for all the things God had done for us and given us.

The party 'programme' was extensive. Georg, our son-in-law, welcomed everyone and explained what would be happening. Elizabeth had devised a children's activity, so next, she spoke about that. There was plenty for the children to find out, including the wide range of nationalities represented at this tea party.

We had some very special music on the keyboard, provided by Isobel, beginning with a hymn of thanksgiving, after which Maurits (married to Anne our granddaughter) spoke about God's faithfulness, based on verses from Lamentations in the Old Testament. There was more of our favourite music throughout the afternoon, including during the eating of English and American cakes, and later during some games. Contributions from children and guests made our day unforgettable. Maurits and Angie (married to Thomas, one of our grandsons) combined their musical talents by singing 'When I'm Ninety-four' (based on the Beatles song, but now with new words!). Maurits, dressed in a bowler hat and smart suit, resembled an English gentleman and amused us by telling jokes about old age. He also sang 'O Sole Mio', which was something we sang at The Mill many years ago.

Another highlight for me was the choice of games. Pass the parcel chocolate game, one of my favourites (when the person has to dress up with hat, scarf and gloves before using a knife and fork to dig into the chocolate bar), was a great success. Musical chairs was also hugely enjoyed and I don't think I need to mention who won that game! Then there was the quiz devised by English friends Isobel, and Dave and Laraine Cook. Rob and I each led a team, with our four grandchildren split between the two of us. The questions were all about America and England with Rob's team just winning by a small margin.

That's what I wanted, a fun party with young and old and everyone in between. A celebration, spanning several nationalities and generations, showing how important family and friends are and also how great God is! What I hadn't reckoned on was just how interested people were in our lives. Both Rob and I felt called to serve God through a ministry which was committed to children. It fills us with joy and pride that people want to hear more of our story. This is our legacy, our story, and we are eager to share it with family, future generations and friends in Austria, England, America and beyond.

Lilian Schunneman

Chapter I

Two Contrasting Childhoods
and Younger Years

Robert's Memories

My Roots

Although from America, I have European roots. My grandfather, Hans Christian Schönemann, came from Schleswig Holstein, then part of Denmark. The border between Germany and Denmark sometimes changed in those days and, interestingly, my ancestors spoke German. In 1880, my grandfather, a cabinetmaker, boarded a ship, together with his wife Anna Marie and one child. Leaving a politically unstable Denmark behind, they felt they were entering the promised land of the US with unlimited personal opportunities. Shortly after they arrived, in 1881 another child was born. Sadly, soon afterwards, Anna Marie died, and my grandfather then married my grandmother Christena, born 1868 in Denmark, who had also settled in the US. From researching family records, it seems that my grandfather changed his surname of Schönemann to Schünemann just before he left Denmark. This was because there was another cabinetmaker in the area with the same name, and he wanted to avoid any confusion. My mother also knew of this fact. My father, John William, was born a Schunneman (without the umlaut and the extra 'n') on 18 December 1904.

My Birth and Early Days

> *I praise you because I am fearfully and wonderfully made, your works are wonderful.*
>
> **Psalm 139 v 14**

I, Robert William, the first son in the Schunneman family, was born on 6 October 1929 in the flat above the local shop. Put more accurately, my birth was in White Lake in South Dakota, in the middle of the prairie. I was eight weeks premature and tiny. My birth was the first miracle in my life as initially, there were no signs of life. The doctor was convinced I would not survive, but the midwife massaged me until my breathing was stable. I weighed only two pounds and showed signs of jaundice. Again, the midwife had a plan and put garlic around my neck, which changed my colour. Gradually, I grew and gained strength, but my father always carried me with a small cushion underneath, to prevent my falling from his arms.

I lived with my family in a small town called White Lake, but there was no lake to be seen. It was a quiet place with a local store, filling station, train station and a grain silo, where farmers from the area could store their harvest. The town was mainly inhabited by German-speaking people. My father worked as a mechanic at the filling station, where often the customers could not afford to pay much, if anything, for repair jobs. He was one of the few men who had a car and he knew how important it was to keep the vehicles running. He loved cars and loved his job. In 1930 we moved south to Platte in South Dakota. Every few years, we would move, depending on where my father got a good job. In Platte, my brothers John Thomas (JT) and Paul (Dickie) were born.

The winter months were often severe with heavy snowfalls. Sometimes, we could walk out of our first-floor windows straight onto the snow. Christmas was my favourite time and my father, strongly influenced by the Danish-German culture of his father (rather than by American cultural traditions), only allowed us to put up the tree on Christmas Eve. When the whole family came to visit, we children let the visitors sleep in our beds while we slept on the floor in the hall. As excited children, we got up early to have a secret view of the presents. Most of the time we got things we really needed like boots or clothes but sometimes there were toys and sweets.

I was particularly fond of and close to my Aunt Irene, who was only six years older than me. She took my hand and walked me to school and back every day when we lived in Sioux City. In 1938 my brother Jimmy was born. A little while later, we moved to Charter Oak, Iowa, where my sister Patricia (Patti) was born. Then, in 1941, we moved to Deadwood, where we lived initially in the house of Auntie

Pauline and Uncle Ike. The latter owned a saloon called 'Bodega Bar' in Taylor Street.

For a job after the school day, I worked and cleaned in a small drugstore, which stocked everything needed for those living in a small town. I learnt from my dad that you can do lots of different jobs. Later, we took up residence in a vacant cabin in Boulder Canyon, belonging to a neighbour who had moved away. It was basic accommodation with neither electricity nor running water. We lived like pioneers, had an old horse, a cow, chickens, turkeys and a dog. Every morning my father got up long before us, to light the fire to heat the hut.

I have good memories of my school days even though, as a family, we moved around a lot. Very special was the time in Boulder Canyon, near Deadwood, 1942/44. My favourite teacher often read to us from *Uncle Tom's Cabin* or *Tom Sawyer* and many other children's books. While she read, we often did puzzles, and I recall these times when I see my great-grandchildren.

A Happy Childhood

These were the years when Europe was involved in World War II. However, things were happening so far away that our lives were not impacted by this war, although we did sometimes hear about what was going on through cinema visits.

I learnt something about planes and flying, since near our house in Deadwood was a US Air Force base. I watched the pilots practising, sometimes flying too low, as when they cut the top off the stately fir tree standing in front of our house. We were amazed but began to recognise the mighty strength of these aircraft.

I love thinking back to the winters we experienced every year. There was always so much snow, and my father used his car as a snow-breaker/plough. It meant getting out of the car every so often and shovelling away the snow, but eventually, our destination was reached. Time flew by, and I soon became a teenager. I worked on a farm to earn a little pocket money. I can recall how awful it once was when I lost my hard-earned dollars on the way home. My day as a cowboy began at four in the morning. I rode the farmer's horse and, along with others, rounded up the cattle ready for milking. At first, we milked by hand, which was very hard work.

Although I didn't have much free time, I enjoyed playing with my brothers and sister, often in the woods. We could all swim, so enjoyed playing in the creek. We built a raft and let ourselves be carried downriver by the water rather like Tom Sawyer. We had lots of adventurous ideas and spent our time creatively. Just occasionally things went wrong, like the time when my brother, Dickie, jumped wildly over a stone and broke his arm. We enjoyed such carefree days during my adolescence, and I am really grateful to God for happy childhood days.

The Schunnemans

My mother and maternal grandmother were women who believed in Jesus, always trying to live their lives according to God's word. Their good example was the reason that I

5

learned about Jesus early in my life and got to know Him as my Saviour. My grandmother, born Lynch, was a godly woman. When I visited her house, we knelt by the bed and prayed together. This made a great impact on my life, and a foundation was laid. This was to influence the rest of my life. There were other opportunities to hear God's word at tent missions, in Sioux City, for example, when born-again Christians told the good news of Jesus Christ. My mother and grandmother accompanied us children to these meetings. I can still remember the fresh smell of the sawdust which had been spread on the ground floor of the tent. We also went to other Christian meetings such as Youth for Christ, of which Billy Graham, the famous preacher, was the director. There, we were encouraged to believe in God and His son Jesus Christ. This message hit me and started to change my life. Although my father considered himself a Christian, he did not seem to live a Christian lifestyle. My grandfather, Hans Schunneman, had died in 1928 before I was born.

During the war, my mother worked to support the family income. Many women did the same, joining the navy or marines or working in factories as they wanted to be useful in times of war. If my mother was ever away, my dad looked after us well, doing the cooking and housework.

Amongst us children, I was the eldest and often the leader. My brother, JT, was the clever one. I told him I had become a Christian, believed in Jesus and was interested in evangelism. I was keen to share my faith and encouraged JT to pray and trust in God. Although my brother didn't speak about his beliefs, I feel sure he did believe in Jesus because his behaviour showed the love that Jesus has for us.

One day, I was playing in the garden of our house in Charter Oak when I felt God speak to me. I was aware that at times I did not always honour God with my language, but on this day, the words from Exodus 20 v 7 became very meaningful to me:

You shall not misuse the name of the Lord your God.

I knew I needed to watch what I said (James 3 vs 9 & 10). From then on, I decided to change. I prayed for forgiveness and promised to be careful about my language in the future. This would become important to me for the rest of my life.

My Time in the Navy

After graduating from high school, I entered the navy in 1948, when I was eighteen years old. All young men had to do national/military service, and I went to bootcamp in San Diego, California, for two months. After that, I went to a navy training centre in Memphis (NATTC), Tennessee. I spent a few months on a special training course as an electrical engineer for aircraft, but I did not complete the course. A friend of our family, a representative in the Congress, knew of an exceptional opportunity in the officer training school (US Naval Academy). I took up this offer and moved to Annapolis, Maryland.

During these two years, we went on a two-month sea trip on a small ship known as a destroyer. Alongside other boats, we were the biggest convoy. We went across the Atlantic, past Scotland to southern Sweden and northern France, where I would later see the devastation caused by WWII. We had weeks of an Atlantic storm so that our convoy had to change course. The large cannons on board meant that there was a real danger of us sinking. A turning angle of forty-five degrees in high waves would have sunk the ships so this was a difficult manoeuvre. One day, the captain allowed me to steer the boat, but I failed miserably, so he resumed the job. I loved life on board as a cadet and think it was the best part of my navy years.

My Quiet Time with God

To be a Christian on board ship required much discipline as we were busy from early in the morning to late in the day. I wanted to serve the Lord with all my love, strength and devotion, so I had to get my priorities right and give Him the best time of the day. For those unfamiliar with the term 'Quiet Time', it is a period of time during the day, often, but not exclusively, in the morning, when individual Christians seek to meet with God through Bible reading and prayer. Reflecting on the passage read, and then praying for themselves and others, helps Christians to maintain a relationship with God amidst their busy lives.

The discipline of having a 'Quiet Time' on board ship became the practice I followed for the rest of my life. It was important to have a firm foundation on which to base my life, especially as there wasn't a firm foundation beneath us out at sea. I got into the habit of setting the alarm clock to 5 a.m. and putting the clock on the other side of the room. That meant I had to get out of bed, and in doing so, became more awake, ready to sit up in bed with my Bible in hand. If the clock had stayed by my bed, I would simply have switched off the alarm and gone back to sleep. Soon, others on board heard I was a Christian, getting up early to pray, so I was then asked by other Christian cadets to wake them up for prayer too. This very personal time with the Lord has always carried me through good but also difficult times.

Our ship docked twice, first, at Gothenburg, south-west Sweden, and then Cherbourg in France. At the latter, I saw for the first time the effects of WWII. The harbour and the surrounding areas were completely destroyed. On board there was good companionship amongst us, and often we had great fun. I didn't mind being out at sea for months, being rocked about. We had to practise using military ammunition, but I'm thankful to God it never came to real military engagement.

Time at the Naval Academy: A New Life Direction Emerges

Two years of my naval time was spent at the Officers' Training Academy in Annapolis, Maryland. There were approximately 1500 cadets in total, split into four classes. We felt very honoured the day President Harry S Truman came for a visit. My impression was that both he and the previous president, Dwight D Eisenhower, were godly men.

One day, when I was standing on the balcony in the large hall, observing the men below eating their meals, I felt God speak to me quite clearly. I was to have a future, as a missionary, working with children. This message was clear, and it made sense. I'd had such a wonderful childhood and loved being around children. It now felt the right time to leave the navy after four years. Fellow cadets knew something had changed. It was God's calling, it was His voice I had heard, and I wanted to follow and be obedient.

California, to Catch Up with Family

By 1952 when I was nearly twenty-three years old, my national service was complete, and I spent time in California with my family who had recently moved there. My father worked as a carpenter and also at a dairy. He got me a temporary job at the latter, washing dairy milk bottles. We often licked the cream left in the containers and enjoyed the ice cream we made. Maybe my father's early death at seventy had something to do with indulging in too much cream and milk products?

My job was only for a short time as I was preparing to go to Bethany Fellowship Missionary Training School in Minneapolis. My parents supported this idea as they were used to my living a distance away from them. Maybe American families are more used to this 'living at a distance' since generations before them got into boats from Europe and landed in the US. Relatives back home were not sure when or if they would see them again. I was to spend three years at Bethany, where I would be prepared for missionary service worldwide. Bethany had been founded by five families from a Norwegian background who had sold their homes and bought a big farm together. Their vision was to teach Christians. I had thoughts about going to work in Ireland but the director of the World Missions to Children, Mr Steele, whom I had met in California, told me my first task was to go to Bethany and receive training in Christian ministry.

Life at Bethany 1952–1955

The training at Bethany was very precious but also quite intensive. Whilst there, I had an experience which shook me deeply, but I have never spoken about this before. We knew that the Bible School director was often called away to an Indian village whose inhabitants believed demons were amongst them. He went and prayed for the people to be saved and be freed from these negative forces. However, it was important for the people themselves to recognise their own need of Jesus Christ, who could set them free. At Bethany, we too sometimes felt we were being spiritually attacked.

My room-mate and I always slept with the window open. Once, I heard a loud, penetrating scream and ran to my colleague's bed as he claimed that something had hit him hard in the stomach. It felt like dark forces were trying to attack us, and we prayed for God's protection. Putting ourselves under the authority and protection of Jesus enabled peace to return to that room. After that, never again did we experience such powerful attacks.

Both the spiritual and the practical experiences were important foundations for future life in missionary service. Our day began at 4.30a.m., with work to do in the different areas before we started classes and were taught. The afternoon was taken up with practical work, and in the evening, we had time for Bible study.

On the practical side, I learned so much, and this was probably the most important preparation for my later ministry at the Schwaigmühle in Austria. For example, I learned everything to do with harvesting sweetcorn, from sowing seeds to selling the product at the weekly market. I helped produce some Norwegian inventions, mostly toys or electric appliances, got experience cutting hair in the salon and also working in the printing office. In fact, the print office had an interesting history. A severe fire, prior to my time at Bethany, had destroyed the original building although the print machines survived. A new and better building had now been erected, which had increased the capacity for printing books. Thanks to the rich blessing of God, following a devastating fire, many world-famous Christian books were now printed here. For example, the Janette Oke series. These books were lovingly called the 'Okey books'. Today they can still be found, translated into many different languages. They are a great testimony of God's love. Whenever I later held a book by Janette Oke, vivid memories of the printing press came back to me.

Due to our work input, the training costs at Bethany were quite low. As far as I can remember, I had to pay a one-time fee of 100 dollars for the three years' training, and any outstanding fees were 'covered' through working on practical initiatives. When the training ended, I was quite sad as I had been so happy there, but I knew I had to move on to the next stage of my life and start work with a missionary society. How would I decide which society and where to go? Over the years, I had heard many presentations from different missionary societies, but one especially came back into mind. That was the World Missions to Children who had projects in several countries. One was a children's home in Ireland. The talk by their director had inspired and encouraged me, so I made an application. I was successful, and my next task was to secure financial support and start a prayer group. Many visits were made to the west coast of the USA, and I was accompanied by Edith Kaufmann, an older Jewish lady, a widow, who was a member of the Mission. Together we looked for financial and prayer support before we embarked on our journey to Drewstown House in Ireland.

Lilian's Memories

Birth and Childhood

On 1 November 1929, I was born into the Keable family, the first of four children. My mother, Grace, was very loving and a devoted housewife, and my father, Robert, worked as a car mechanic in a local garage. I spent the first eleven years of my life living at 14, Aitken Road, Catford, south-east London. Robertson's jam factory was in the immediate vicinity and offered many jobs to local people. In 1931 my brother Robert was born, followed by Beryl in 1934 and June in 1936.

My memories of childhood are hazy, but I remember good playtimes with the many children who lived on our road. Roller skates and bicycles were borrowed and we raced around at breakneck speed. Not surprising then, was a visit to hospital following a laceration over my right eye and subsequent stitches. As children, we were inventive, making things for play. I was sometimes called a 'tomboy' as my skirt did not prevent me from climbing successfully onto boys' bikes; a lively girl who didn't think about the conventions of gender roles. Favourite games were 'Whip and Top', 'Hopscotch' and 'Cowboys and Indians'.

Aged five, I walked to school a short distance away but in rainy weather, we took the tram. As was usual in England at the time, our parents sent us to Sunday school at a local church. Although they didn't attend church themselves, they thought it important for us to be there. We four children heard stories from the Bible every week, though I have no real memories of Sunday school.

World War II Reaches London

After some carefree years, the impact of war reached us and all those with a garden in London, in our case, a backyard, had to dig a protective bunker. The hole, a few square metres in size, was lined with a metal casing and covered with earth. A steep earth path led down to the bunker, and when the siren sounded, we hurried there and huddled together. Bomb attacks by the Germans were often at night, but also during the day when we sat for hours in darkness. It was a basic refuge with hard wooden benches, and I can't remember if we kept food and blankets there. We also had an 'outhouse' which served as a toilet, but that didn't give much space as we also kept our suitcases in there, ready for a potential evacuation or escape. It wasn't until we heard the special siren sound indicating 'All Clear', that we could go back into the house. Families without a bunker were required to rush to their nearest Underground station for shelter. Sometimes they had to sleep on the train platform all night and this must have been terrifying. Since there was no subway station near us, people without a garden simply had to stay in their homes.

The war impacted our lives more and more. School was problematic, with large classes and insufficient teachers. Then our father was drafted into the 'war service' whilst women without children could volunteer for the 'war effort'. These women stayed at home to support the soldiers. My father drove a truck for the Royal Air Force, transporting aircraft parts, weapons and ammunition. He was rarely at home any more, as he travelled all over England, experiencing an involvement in the war effort. My mother supported the four of us by herself.

From London to Willoughby, 1940–1945

One day in summer 1940, my father came home with a plan. He had had enough of the protective bunker in our garden, so we gathered our basic belongings together and left London. Our family of six, plus Aunt Violet ('Vi' as we called her), my mother's twin sister and her son, climbed into our vehicle. My uncle was absent, being on the front line in the war.

What I did not know then was that my father had received a 'tip-off' that London was soon to be heavily bombed. He wanted safety for his family, so without any questions, we just obeyed. As we travelled out of London, northwards, we saw many terrible things: destroyed houses, places on fire, soldiers. This was no family outing; it was our evacuation. Finally, we reached our destination: Willoughby, a rural village, north-west of London. This place had never been the target of bombing. The nearest towns were Rugby and Coventry. We were met by Mr Harding, the 'billeting officer' of the village. He was responsible for ensuring evacuees found shelter with rural families, but this wasn't easy for us, since we were so many. We were sent to the nearby village of Braunston where there was a 'country club'; essentially a house but also a hotel. An old lady resided there, but from the outset, my mother felt there was something not quite right about this situation. She even wondered if the bombings' atmosphere in London might be preferable to this place. We only stayed briefly, having heard the lady wandering around in the night waiting for guests who never came. We left and made our way back to Mr Harding, a member of the Methodist church and a farmer. He graciously allowed us to stay with him at his farm, the 'White House', until we could find another place. Looking back, I see God's guidance against a chaotic background of the war.

Mr Harding lived with his two employees, the housekeeper and the maid, in one part of the house, while the seven of us lived in the other (my father had returned to military service). There was a small Methodist chapel in the village, and the farmer was responsible for holding a service there on Sundays. Guest preachers were invited and out of gratitude for a roof over our heads, my mother and her sister attended. Whilst I can't say they accepted Jesus as their Saviour, I do know that during this time, Jesus Christ became very important to me.

War causes people to ask questions such as 'Where is God?'. Some can't understand why God allows these horrors to happen whilst others believe trustingly because they know that God is their protection. Even in exceptional circumstances like this, when I cannot understand such situations, I stand with those who can testify that the Lord is faithful.

War Impacts our Lives

My father was proved right, and a few weeks after we arrived at Willoughby, 'The Blitz' came over London. Hitler's Luftwaffe bombed and destroyed vast areas of the city. Between autumn 1940 and early summer 1941, more than 40,000 people, mainly civilians, fell victims to 'The Blitz'. For me, the worst night of this time was 14 November 1940. At 7.30p.m., the German Air Force began 'Operation Moonlight Sonata' and attacked the city of Coventry from the air. This was not far from Willoughby. Coventry, an important industrial site, known for its metal and ammunition factories, had a population of approximately 300,000. Tens of thousands of civilians inevitably fell victim to these attacks, dying or seriously injured.

We were terrified that our village would also be attacked, and when we heard the bombs falling nearby, we huddled together under the kitchen table as there was no shelter on the farm. It is thanks to God's protection and grace that we remained unharmed, and not a single bomb fell on Willoughby. Life had to go on, and gradually we felt safer. We attended a small village school where the classes were amalgamated. In spite of all the difficulties, my mother coped well with life in a new place. We siblings kept busy playing, in winter, skating on the frozen pond and playing ice hockey, making our own sticks. In summer, we climbed trees and swung like Tarzan from branch to branch. Foodwise, fresh bread was scarce, and we children loved the crusty bits. My mother divided pieces up between us four children.

The war was not far away, and more evacuees came to Willoughby. I'm ashamed to recall that at times we children considered the newcomers as intruders into our village. All too soon we had forgotten that we, too, were evacuees and had been received mercifully. The parsonage housed Jews from Vienna, who had fled from Nazi Germany. The children from those families joined in our playtimes.

My Encounter with Jesus

During the war, the 'Non-Combatant Corps' existed. These were groups of older Christian men, many above recruitment age, who did not want to carry weapons or be involved in the war. The Government accepted this stance, but in return, these men were required to participate in some kind of community service. They worked in a depot, and their task was to ensure that those on the front line of the war received such items as blankets, fresh uniforms, food, weapons, etc. In addition, they did practical work on farms, supporting families when the resident farmer and his male helpers were away fighting.

It so happened that one of these 'Non-Combatant Corps' was stationed at Barby, a village close to Willoughby. We saw some of these men on Sundays, when our host, Mr Harding, invited them to come and lead a service in our local Methodist chapel. They joined us for a snack afterwards. They also held children's meetings during the week, which I attended. It was thanks to these men that I heard the Gospel and got to know the Bible better. The Christian songs we sang really 'spoke' to me about the love of God; His promises remain the same in war, in peacetime, in suffering, in sickness and in death. These years at Willoughby shaped the rest of my life. God holds the greater picture of our lives which we will never see while we are on earth.

The foundation on which my ninety-year-old legs still stand today, is simply that God is good and His promises do not fail. This is the cornerstone of my faith and my firm certainty.

Serious Illness

In October 1942, aged thirteen, I was taken to hospital having suffered with severe pain for several days. The medics diagnosed a ruptured appendix and an emergency operation took place as my life was in danger. The operation went well, but there was insufficient penicillin for the post-operative treatment. The supplies were reserved for soldiers fighting on the front line, so it meant that I had to stay in hospital for some time. Then I got peritonitis which led to two more operations. A colostomy bag (linked to an opening in the bowel) enabled my colon to recover whilst I was fed intravenously through a cannula in my legs. With so few painkillers available, morphine was prescribed.

I did not understand the danger I was in, but my mother was fully aware. For the first six critical weeks, she took the bus every evening, covering an eight-mile journey, so that she could sit with me overnight. She was afraid I might die alone, as very few medical staff were available with only one nurse on duty at night. Meanwhile, back at Willoughby, my Aunt Vi looked after the children.

Following surgery, I could only take liquid foods but gradually things began to improve. Then, when I was nearly fourteen, another operation successfully removed the colostomy bag and joined the two sections of the colon together again. My digestion returned to normal. My mother regularly brought in a basket full of food and, on Sundays, there was the treat of roast beef, Yorkshire pudding and vegetables. These were kept warm by hot water bottles placed under the pots. However, whilst my appetite improved, my abdominal wound was slow to heal. A Czech doctor prescribed a paste for my stomach, meaning my belly was creamed and bandaged. Over time there was gradually healing.

Gratitude and a Promise to God

During my fourteen months in the hospital, I began to think more deeply about God and His purposes for my life. A desire emerged in me, to give something back to God as He had preserved my life. I felt called into missionary service, and to live my life totally for Him.

Back 'home' at Willoughby in November 1943, more illness struck me with the onset of rheumatic fever. It was back to bed for rest, followed by short journeys around the farm in a wheelchair which had been purchased for me. A pair of binoculars enabled me to do some birdwatching and trainspotting. At times, it was very frustrating having to rely on others to push me around in the wheelchair but I soon, with much determination, moved myself with my feet. I also read about five books a week, for example, *Anne of Green Gables*, *Tom Sawyer* and *Uncle Tom's Cabin*. Once more, I recovered from illness and was yet again grateful to God.

End of War in Sight

In 1944, my father had to go to the front in France and not long after, we experienced the 'D-Day Landings'. This was one of the key events of World War II along with 'Operation Overlord' or the 'Allied Invasion'. My father was one of those soldiers of the 'second front'. After this invasion had succeeded, the end of the war seemed foreseeable. We remained in Willoughby until the war with Japan was over.

In August 1945, after my brother had finished the school year, we returned to London. My mother got a job at Robertson's jam factory, close to my Aunt Vi and other relations. It was in that area we found an affordable rental property. More women, often widows, were now taking jobs to provide for themselves and their families.

The long period of rebuilding our country began. It was a time of recovery, but it took decades for families to cope with the loss of their men. Women and children suffered in particular, but there was also an impact on industry and the world of work.

We lost our father but not through war. In 1947, he returned from military service and rather than coming back to live with us, he went to live with his mother. We never knew why, and contact stopped. It was particularly difficult for me as I had done so much with him. In fact, I discovered my love of sport through going to football, tennis and cricket matches with him. My brother Robert took on the role of 'man in the family' and was a great support to my mother until her death. My father died in autumn 1950, aged forty-four, from aplastic anaemia. I was twenty then and only managed to visit him once. The pastor of my church visited him in hospital and reported that my father had said, 'If God is on my side, nothing can happen to me'. I don't know if this meant he had made a commitment to be with the Lord or not, but obviously I hope so. Only God knows the hearts of men and women. It was a devastating time for me, but I picked myself up and tried to resume my life.

Way back then, there was no understanding of this illness, but my father's job had entailed delivering ammunition containing chemicals. As there was no protective clothing, we can only assume that his 'exposure' to these chemicals was the cause of his untimely death. We were just one of many families who lost men in similar circumstances.

My Decision to Follow Jesus

Back in March 1945, I made a conscious decision to follow Christ. I accepted Him as my personal Lord and Saviour, having confessed my sins to Him. Did a serious change in my life follow? Yes, because I now realised what was right and wrong before God.

I have swept away your offences like a cloud, your sins like the morning mist. Return you to me, for I have redeemed you.

Isaiah 44 v 22

This was engraved on my mind, and I did not want to be like others. After the war, there was much celebration. Young people, in particular, went to lots of parties, drank heavily and danced wildly, celebrating the return of men from war. I wanted to live my life in a different way, so my time was frequently spent with friends from church. This had a positive effect on my life, and in 1946 I was baptised.

Education and Work

Having been in hospital for so long, I had missed out on my school education and was unable to return to the regular school system. To make up for this deficit, I attended night school, alongside a day job in the office of a forwarding agency. My aunt helped me get this job, and then my uncle helped me secure a job at United Dairies where I worked in their accounts department until 1950. I was good with maths, checking numbers of bottles of milk delivered by milk suppliers through their registration books, against the total quantities of milk delivered to customers. This prevented any supplier from misappropriating milk bottles.

Meanwhile, my brother Robert started an apprenticeship in the air force aged sixteen and later became a firefighter. He pursued his job with passion until his retirement. I must confess that in my youth I did not think much about my mother and siblings. It never occurred to me to stay at home to help my mother or keep her company. My brother was different and exercised great responsibility. I, on the other hand, spent a lot of time with friends from the Bermondsey Gospel Mission Church, where I was a member.

My Church Family

Ted Preston, one of the soldiers who preached at Willoughby, had told me about the Bermondsey church. I felt very much part of the church family and was friendly with Ruth Bustin, the daughter of the superintendent of the church. We were the same age and did a lot of things together. One day she wanted me to go to the cinema with her to see a ballet film. Whilst her pocket money exceeded my wages from the dairy, I knew that if I joined her, my entire weekly allowance would be gone in one night. I was talked into this frivolity, came to regret it very much and firmly resolved never to do anything like that again. Only the 'upper class' could afford this kind of entertainment, and I resigned myself to the fact I did not belong.

We young people at the church did a lot together. We had outings to the park, seaside, picnics, and enjoyed sport. On weekday evenings, there was a Bible study or prayer meeting. Sunday services happened both morning and evening, with Sunday school in the afternoon. I regularly helped with the children's programme, as well as attending the church services. As I got older, I realised that I should be at home with my mother more often, so I stayed with her on Sunday mornings.

My Way to Bible College

It was my heart's desire to get to know the Bible better in order to lay a more solid foundation for later service in mission. Finding the right college would not be difficult since few took women. The choice was: Mount Hermon, Ridgelands Bible College or Redcliffe College and I chose the latter. The college had been recommended to me by my church family and was located at Chiswick, west of London. The fees were £25 per term, so I saved money from my wages to pay for the first term. My church also generously donated funds, and I worked during the holidays until I finally had all the money together. God always provided me with everything I needed. My mother supported my project and accepted my path in life. My sisters both got married young and, together with their husbands, had differing interests to me. Nevertheless, our relationship has always been intimate and loving, and we always kept connected.

Redcliffe College, 1950–1952: My First Impressions

I found college life very strict. Previously, I had been able to choose what I wanted to do, but here, I began to miss my church friends very much. There were rules about how to wear your hair and uniform. The principal was responsible for making sure that everything was done correctly. If rules were disregarded, then we were called to her 'to have a little word'. It's still in my ear today, 'Do you need a little word?'. We were reproached for mistakes and warned to behave differently in future. As the weeks passed and the December end of term was approaching, I wished, on occasions, that I would be told not to return because I had not passed the probationary period.

Daily Life

In total, we were thirty students and mealtimes presented particular challenges. There were six tables, five of which were presided over by a member of staff and one by the principal. British table manners of the time were required, meaning that you did not help yourself to food, but waited for your neighbour on your left to offer you the serving dishes. The aim of this was to ensure you waited in a well-behaved manner, and also that you took care of your neighbour sitting on your right. It often happened that under the table, one stepped on the shin of the left neighbour as a reminder to pass food. One day a student stepped accidentally on the shin of the principal having noticed too late who she was kicking. I wonder if that action then required 'a little word'. Today it makes me laugh to recall this, but in those days, it was no laughing matter. On the subject of food, there was never any discussion as to whether we liked the food or not. Our motto was, 'What He gives me I will swallow, where He leads, I will follow'. We had already heard that in Brazil, monkeys' eyes were served as a delicacy, or some fish had to be swallowed with all the trimmings.

Every day, after lunch, we had to take a prescribed walk, not only with a fellow student we knew well, but sometimes with others we didn't know or particularly like. It had to be a different person each time. Some female students had held senior positions in their jobs prior to college, so our backgrounds were wide-ranging. I tried very hard to get along with everyone and had many friends. At first, it was rather strange when someone came up to me and asked if I would join her on a walk. Very soon we became used to this 'daily duty', and if it turned out to be a walk with someone with whom there was a misunderstanding, things got cleared up quickly. It became clear why we had been given this task: it was to serve as preparation for our missionary service in foreign lands. We were required to respect opinions and to be sensitive to others' values.

We also learned sewing and cooking and many other useful skills that would help make mission life easier. We had to be prepared to be sent out to a place for several years and take care of ourselves.

College Life gets Better

The Christmas holidays passed and no one had told me not to return to college. To my surprise the next year was much easier. I learned that despite all the rigour and discipline, we could have fun, even with the teaching staff. I remembered a mishap happening in the kitchen: we forgot the sugar in the apple pie. I had the simple idea of putting sweetener pills into the ventilation holes on top of the pastry. No one had noticed and the taste was just the same!

The general enthusiasm of both teachers and students for our common good enabled a positive atmosphere to prevail. Finally, a beautiful feeling of belonging to this community filled my heart. Spiritual development happened through Bible study, and we learned many verses off by heart. Sometimes, we recited whole chapters to each other to enhance memory. I memorised the entire Epistle to the Ephesians, and several chapters of the book of Daniel, and I can still recall these long passages today. Each day we had a 'Quiet Time' before breakfast, a practice which has remained with me, though sometimes the timing has changed. The ruling in college was that following the Quiet Time, our rooms had to be tidied before we came down to breakfast.

After breakfast, various household or kitchen duties had to be performed, followed by a prayer time for the whole community. Then lessons took place until lunchtime. Post lunch, there was the obligatory walk, already mentioned, and in the afternoon, we helped with different Christian programmes outside college. In neighbouring churches, opportunities abounded to help with children's work, women's classes and other Christian activities. After our evening meal, we had personal study time until bedtime around 9.30p.m. Saturday was our day off when I cycled about fourteen miles to visit my family. Sundays were busy with church services in different places.

Everything is Easier with Humour

Every year, England celebrates a spectacular military parade, 'Trooping the Colour'. It's in honour of Queen Elizabeth II's birthday and takes place on Horse Guards Parade, London. The Queen receives the 'Royal Salute' as the flag is hoisted, and then, on horseback, she inspects her troops. After that, individual troop units march past the Queen, accompanied by military bands. Even if you haven't seen this ceremony, I hope you will understand what I now describe.

Everyone at college knew I was an admirer of the Queen, a fact that is still the case today. As a true Londoner, I watched this ceremony close up on several occasions, and was a true patriot. So, on Friday, 27 June 1952, I had the crazy idea of re-enacting this event in college. This was just a few weeks after the real Trooping of the Colour, but instead of calling it 'Trooping the Colour', we called it 'Drooping the Colour'. The word 'drooping' means withering. No sooner said than done. Many student colleagues joined in on the idea, and were ready to take on acting roles. Some students 'became' soldiers by putting buckets or wastepaper baskets on their heads and waved umbrellas as 'rifles'. My bicycle 'became' a horse by means of a cardboard box (head) and a brush (tail). It didn't take much effort for me to mime the Queen, so I sat on my horse and waved at everyone. A bucket on my head served as my crown, and the red lining of my jacket was the perfect royal cape. And so, I rode through a trellis of umbrellas and let my subjects celebrate me as their monarch. We laughed until we cried.

Living at Redcliffe College gave us a great vantage point for the annual Oxford v Cambridge Boat Race. We were close to the finishing line, and stood on a bridge to catch sight of the two rowing teams.

My Pioneers and Role Models

During my youth and whilst at college, I loved to read and hear about some great pioneers who served God in different parts of the world. Here, I will mention briefly six individuals who truly inspired me. Hopefully, you will be encouraged to read their biographies.

James Hudson Taylor, 1832–1905: was born in England and felt called to China where he spent fifty-one years. He became known as a 'pioneer in the forbidden land'. The China Inland Mission was founded by him.

Jim Elliot, 1927–1956: was an American who worked among the Huaorani people (Auca) in Ecuador. In 1956, along with some friends, he was killed by the Indians. But that wasn't 'the end' of his story.

Charles T Studd, 1860–1931: was born in England and felt called to China. Later, he pastored a church in India, followed by work in Africa. He founded a movement which became known as WEC (World Evangelisation Crusade).

Mary Mitchell Slessor, 1848–1915: was born in Britain and worked in Nigeria, caring for twin babies, then considered to be a curse. She saved the lives of many children.

Gladys May Aylward, 1902–1970: was an English missionary who worked in China with orphans during the Sino-Japanese war.

Amy Carmichael, 1867–1951: was an English woman who felt called to India, where she cared for thousands of children and founded orphanages.

We students at Redcliffe learned so much from these pioneers and wanted to take them as our role models. Interestingly, women had a key role on the mission field at this time in history, serving faithfully and selflessly until they died. We often heard the call from the mission field: 'We need a man, send me a woman'. Nurses were in great demand as were doctors, midwives, surgeons, teachers and cooks. There were examples where women carried huge responsibilities and excelled in their roles under God's blessing. Sometimes their work was not recognised until after their death, as was the case with one college friend who worked in Nepal as a doctor in hugely challenging circumstances. She was honoured posthumously by the Royal College of Surgeons. All were an inspiration to us in different ways and I, personally, felt called to work in India or Nigeria. I was convinced this was the path for me. Meanwhile, a group of seven of us at college were particular friends and have remained so over the years until death parted us. Five of us went into full-time mission, and two stayed in England.

For a missionary, it's not about seeking success or gaining honour; it is simply that whatever we achieve, is actually what God has enabled us to do in His service. When we feel unable to do tasks that we believe God has called us to do, then we pray even more. If God leads us, then He will equip us. I had decided to follow Jesus. He had given His life for me, so I was giving my life back to Him. My dream was to go to a foreign country and give a home to children who had to be kept apart from parents infected by leprosy. These children needed care, and I felt this could be where God wanted to place me.

Extension of College Time

At the end of my second year, the principal, who despite her severity forever holds a special place in my heart, invited me to spend the summer holidays helping to harvest fruit and vegetables, assisted by some teachers. Since I had not planned anything else, I accepted. It was the custom that each year a student would be asked to do this. So, during the summer, I harvested and cooked. A tenth of this produce was put aside and was later given away at the harvest festival in the autumn. Often these gifts went to a children's home. Many Christians believe that giving a 'tithe' (a tenth) is a biblical principle. We give back to the Lord a portion of what we have received from Him.

Post-College Hopes and Plans

I was twenty-three when my time at Redcliffe College finished, and I returned home wondering what to do next. My desire to serve the Lord in India or Africa remained. Little did I know that 'God's place' would actually be Austria. I was very clear about my mission calling, and I was equally clear, from early on in life, that I wanted to work with children. This idea of working with children was not a sudden whim. God gave me some verses repeatedly over the years that confirmed this vocation.

Then Pharaoh's daughter went down to the Nile to bathe, and her attendants were walking along the riverbank. She saw the basket among the reeds and sent her female slave to get it. She opened it and saw the baby. He was crying, and she felt sorry for him. 'This is one of the Hebrew babies,' she said. Then his sister asked Pharaoh's daughter, 'Shall I go and get one of the Hebrew women to nurse the baby for you?' 'Yes, go,' she answered. So the girl went and got the baby's mother. Pharaoh's daughter said

to her, 'Take this baby and nurse him for me, and I will pay you.'
So, the woman took the baby and nursed him.

Exodus 2 vs 5-9

This story describes how Moses was rescued. In my missionary life, I would take care of children, not rewarded by payment, but by God blessing my life.

Training to Become a Nursery Nurse, 1952–1954

So, without further ado, I decided to train as a nursery nurse, that is both a nursery school teacher and a children's nurse. In a hospital setting at this time, a nursery nurse would support the new mother in teaching her skills in handling a new baby. In other settings, a nursery nurse might work in a children's home or be employed as a nanny in a particular family. In England, it was, and still is, the custom for very rich people to employ a nanny. The training for a nursery nurse lasted two years. The first year I spent in Rugby, living with a family. It was an ideal placement as there were no fees involved, and the location was one I remembered from our days in the evacuation. My second year was spent at Tapeley Park in Devon, and there is much to recall about my time there.

Life at Tapeley Park

Tapeley Park was a very large mansion, with extensive grounds, owned privately by a famous family called Christie. During the Second World War, the building had been opened for social purposes, and an orphanage was temporarily established there. The gardens were beautiful giving a wonderful view of the sea. Working there brought me a number of benefits, not least because I did not have to pay any training expenses. I could complete my vocational training and gain additional work experience.

The children in the orphanage were taken on walks around the gardens every day. My notebook, which went with me everywhere, enabled me to record key information: the food children had eaten, appointments with doctors, medication given. I meticulously recorded all the details. Each employee had a specific child to care for, and I was given David. He became very special to me, and to this day, I wonder what happened to him. I even hoped that he might be adopted into my own family. Aunt Joan, my late father's sister, offered to take in David, but he was not offered up for adoption. Coming to terms with this was hard, but while David was in my care, he was looked after very well. Night shifts were also part of our training, and the time was usually spent ironing. Sometimes, we workers competed to see who could iron more shirts in an hour. This was an incentive to work fast, and the night passed more quickly.

Into Employment at the Royal Free Hospital, 1954–1956

For a long time, this hospital, founded in 1828, was the only one where women could receive medical training and provided for those who could not afford medical treatment. I enjoyed working there, at first in the maternity department, and then later on the children's ward.

Whilst working on the infant ward, I got unspeakable pain in my back. A consultant at the hospital examined me and diagnosed a kidney stone. Immediately, an operation took place, and I had the luxury of being given a private room in which to recover. However, as I gradually got better, it was time to face a devastating realisation: my plan to work in Nigeria or India was crumbling. I was told that my health would not stand up to living in hot climates, with challenging conditions. My 'dream' of many years had died, but as yet, I didn't know that God had assigned me a different task.

This was a life with a man I was yet to meet, and with whom I would have a beautiful daughter. I would have a family life, experience community, and still be able to fulfil my missionary vocation. Many women I knew in missionary service had remained unmarried, believing they could then concentrate more fully on their work. Others who married, had a family and worked overseas, found they had to return home once the children were of school age so that their children's education would not suffer.

My final exams took place in Bristol. I then prayed for God to reveal a new plan for my life. I began to realise that when God closes one door, He opens another.

Chapter 2

Two Paths Cross in Ireland

As the heavens are higher than the earth, so are my ways higher than your ways and my thoughts than your thoughts.

Isaiah 55 v 9

Robert's Memories, 1956–1958

About thirty children resided at Drewstown House. It was a large property with many outbuildings and extensive grounds. The Mission policy was that only Protestant children were accepted and similar Catholic institutions took in children from their faith. Although there were clear divisions between Protestants and Catholics in Ireland, fortunately in everyday life it was less noticeable.

From the outset, I felt very much at home in Ireland, perhaps because my maternal grandparents were from there and the 'Irishness' was in my genes. My ancestors belonged to those Irish emigrants who had left for the USA in the nineteenth century to escape the great famine.

Daily Life

My daily practical tasks were varied but strategic in keeping the buildings in good order. Maintaining an effective heating system was a challenge but the director, Bob Minter, had a brilliant idea, and I was responsible for sorting a practical solution. The oven was heated up by making a fire, giving out a high temperature very quickly. However, after the initial burst of heat, the oven rapidly cooled down and some rooms became cold. Bob's idea was to create a conveyor belt in front of the oven, which automatically added sawdust. Possibly this was the first woodchip plant in the world, and it's a pity we didn't apply for a patent!

One of my biggest challenges on the practical side was digging a well. In the middle of winter, after intensive digging to about eight metres, lasting over several months, I eventually struck water. Pure drinkable water! Fortunately, for further work, I had help, or rather I sorted my own assistance. Workers were laying gas pipes on our property, and at night their tractor stood abandoned. I am not proud of my actions, but I 'borrowed' this useful vehicle. There were no keys, but I got the thing running, and lowered round concrete rings into the well. These soon filled with clean water. A guilty conscience hung over me, but I would not have succeeded in my task without this heavy equipment. However, all this taught me a hard lesson. If you get pure water from a well, you must never disturb the well. Sometime later, we had to move the well because of a regulation, and we temporarily lost our water supply. We did locate it some metres away, but it was never as clear as before. This incident taught me how precious it is to have pure water and to be able to keep it.

Chickens were kept on our land but they were not laying eggs regularly, and were very messy creatures. From my childhood experiences, I knew how to look after these creatures. I used sawdust in their sheds and closed the doors to keep the warmth in. This resulted in a good supply of eggs thus pleasing the kitchen staff, the hungry children and the employees. Tending the garden was also my responsibility, and the use of a shotgun kept thieving birds at bay.

Each day, I took the children to school. On the staff was Lilian Keable, a young woman who helped with the girls. We got along well and had some good conversations. On some occasions, the children were taken on outings, and once, in Dublin, a woman stopped me in the street, asking if all the children belonged to me. When I explained they were from a children's home, she was visibly relieved and crossed herself.

A Romance Begins

I have already mentioned Lilian, a charming and bright young lady. And so it was that our friendship developed over many months. One very special evening, we drove to an evangelistic meeting in the staff car. Both of us were sitting in the back, and I felt deep down that my interest in Lil was growing. It was a mutual feeling. I knew she was 'the one' for me and would become Mrs Schunneman. I held her hand and put my arm around her shoulder. Although from this point we 'belonged' to each other, our plan was to make good use of our time together at Drewstown and get to know each other better. It was not a situation to rush, and also important to set a good example to the children in our care.

We talked much about where we might serve God together; Lil saw her destiny in Salzburg, Austria. I remained unsure for a while. But as so often is the case (I say this with a smile on my face), 'she always lets me go her way, she always wins'. Soon, God made it clear to us both that Austria was where we would find our joint destiny.

In 1958, my time at Drewstown House came to an end. Overall, I had not seen much of Ireland, as we were there to work. Many years later, a little after our fiftieth wedding anniversary, my brother Jimmy and his wife took us back to Ireland where we toured the country and visited Drewstown.

Lilian's Memories, 1956–1957

My dream of helping children in tropical countries had vanished into thin air, and I wondered what plan God had for me. My dear friend Barbara Simpson, whom I knew from my time at Redcliffe College, and her husband, Brian, worked in Salzburg with the Slavic Gospel Association. They were ministering to some of the Displaced Persons from Eastern Europe. In our correspondence, she told me about the World Missions to Children which had workers in Salzburg. They were caring for children, now orphans[1], whose birth parents were African American occupation soldiers and young

---

[1] Sources estimate there were around 30,000 children thought to have been fathered by Allied soldiers in Austria post WWII. About 350-400 of these children had Afro-American fathers. Due to the complex political and social situation at the time, many of these children were given up by their Austrian mothers.

Austrian women. There were ten infants in total, from babies to three years, and more staff were needed to take care of them. The couple in charge were Mr and Mrs Bob Minter, who were shortly due to take leave. My friends the Simpsons, mentioned above, stepped in for a few months to help with the children until Joe and Lee Coulson arrived in August. The Minters left Austria in April 1956 and were visiting England en route for America. That gave me an opportunity to meet up with them in London so they could tell me more about the Mission and the children's work in Salzburg. After our conversation, my interest was sparked to join the Mission. I followed the advice of Mr Ellsworth Steele, the founder of the Mission, applied, and was accepted. The plan was to go to Drewstown House in Ireland. This would be for a few months of probationary training. Mr and Mrs Steele would be present during my time there before they departed for India. I was due in Ireland from October 1956, so until that time, I continued to work as a nurse at the Royal Free.

Daily Life

My training as a nursery nurse was hardly in demand at Drewstown. The focus of my work was housekeeping: planning menus, ordering food, cooking, cleaning and laundry. I spent a lot of time hanging wet laundry in the boiler room where it dried very speedily. A friendly employee, named Robert Schunneman, was often in there ensuring the firewood was in plentiful supply. He skilfully mounted a long clothesline on a movable rack which was a great help in drying all the children's clothes. There was a large entrance hall in the house, with stairs, and I took pride in making sure the floor was regularly scrubbed and polished. It was the first area people saw when they entered the house, and I liked it kept in pristine condition. Cleanliness was always important to me.

We were blessed to have a garden surrounding the house, with chickens providing fresh eggs daily. Although the food we served was simple, we provided good nutritious meals based on a few ingredients and a very limited amount of money.

Two helpers, John and Elena, had responsibility for the children, but on their days off I was given responsibility for the girls, and Rob, for the boys. At first, neither of us thought that this occasional joint working would have a decisive influence on our later lives. I remember that the children in the home were often sad, and I could see this in their eyes. Although they had all the necessities of life, they still lacked that 'parental bond'. One young boy got so excited when his mother came to visit but was so disturbed when she left. We wondered if it would be better for him not to have any future visits, but how can that suggestion be explained to a little boy? Another sad situation was when two sisters lost their mother and their father remarried, with the new wife not wanting the girls. It was hard to watch these young children wrestling with such issues at such a young age.

Each Sunday we took the children to the local Church of Ireland. Everyone was most friendly to us, offering cups of tea after the service. The Irish often drank their tea black and strong and our staff, who were of American origin, were more used to weak tea. The Irish joked that Americans would only drink 'Three Leaf Tea' or 'Lighthouse Tea' ('because it's blinking near water').

Love at Second Glance

I have already mentioned Rob Schunneman and our growing attachment to each other. It would be an exaggeration to say it was love at first sight. Not for me and not for him. I would rather compare our love to a small seed that God had planted in our hearts and nurtured. Little by little, the love grew and became stronger over time. Our comradeship became a good acquaintance, then that became a close friendship, and finally, it turned into deep love. This love for each other remains and is deeply rooted in our hearts today.

We spent Christmas 1957 together in London with my mother, and in January 1958, I went to Austria, where we did not meet again until October. Rob was comfortable with my family, but we couldn't as yet make any firm plans together. He returned to Ireland to continue his work. How it would go with us, we did not know.

Chapter 3

A New Life Begins – The Schwaigmühle

Ruth replied, 'Don't urge me to leave you or to turn back from you. Where you go, I will go, and where you stay I will stay. Your people will be my people and your God my God.'

Ruth 1 v 16

Lilian's Memories

In January 1958 the time had come for me to leave for Austria, where I was already expected by Joseph and Aurelia Coulson. Joseph, originally from the US, was always known as Joe, and Aurelia, known as Lee. She came from Vienna. They lived in a house in St. Jakob near Salzburg, where they took care of the ten orphan children.

For my first six months in Austria, I lived in Salzburg, halfway up the road to the castle, on Oskar-Kokoschka-Weg. Here, I lodged with Frau Wöss from Germany. Her Austrian husband had died in the war on the Russian border, and after his death, she inherited the house on the Mönchsberg, which was called Pension Wöss, a large house below the Festung Hohensalzburg Castle. I lived here during the week and visited the Coulsons and the children on Tuesdays and at weekends. Life in Austria was very different, and I was quite lonely. The Coulsons had each other for company, and I didn't like to bother them about anything. Fortunately, prior to coming to Austria, I had experienced life away from my own family when at Bible College and, later, training in the hospital.

Wait and Hope

I hoped that Rob would join me at some point, but when? I only heard from him very occasionally, and every day when the post arrived, I eagerly awaited a letter. Even Frau Wöss's daughter, Christiane, noticed how sad I was when none arrived and tried to comfort me by saying, 'Perhaps he is simply lazy about writing'. Later, I was to learn the real reason for his not being able to write. It was a difficult time as there were no firm plans between us, but I trusted God that He had prepared the right future for us. However, when I saw the orphan children, they were a real tonic, distracting me and helping me around the house. On Sundays, we took the children to church in Salzburg, which was a great highlight for them as they met others of their own age. Some of the Salzburg residents looked surprised as we walked about town with dark-skinned children.

During the week, I helped Frau Wöss with cleaning and shopping, carrying the bags up and down the steep incline to the house. My biggest challenge was to learn the German language, which Frau Wöss taught me, giving me daily practice in conversation. She would later also teach Rob, and continued as our teacher until about 1962. To this day, we still have contact with her daughter, Christiane, who was a teenager at the time.

From Salzburg, I moved out to St. Jakob and thought this place was the end of the world! It was so quiet, and a complete contrast to the city. But it only took a few weeks before I accepted this small village as my home. I took the children into my heart. With mixed parentage, life was not easy for them. They had been deserted by parents, but the reasons were complicated, and we did not want to make a judgement on their situation. In spite of everything, they were happy children who played, sang and led a carefree life. They had excellent care from the Coulsons. These ten special children were: Eveline, Robert, Margarete, Gerti, Wilma, Josef, twins Peter and Fritzi, Betty and Eduard.

Nevertheless, it soon became clear that the house we all lived in was too small. We looked for a larger property and visited the Schwaigmühle[2], in Großgmain in 1958. It was an ideal property. Joe had good commercial skills, and a contract was duly signed. The authorities were pleased that the orphan children were receiving good care. Our friend Edna joined our team. The Coulsons and the rest of us put all the money we received as individual support into the house. We then agreed on $12 pocket money to cover our monthly

---

[2] Schwaigmühle – *Schwaig* is a German word, referring to a special form of settlement, usually that of farming in Alpine regions; *Mühle* is a German word, meaning mill. The Schwaigmühle was often known as The Mill.

personal expenses. So, all our income was pooled together as a contribution to the renovation and maintenance of the Schwaigmühle.

Robert's Memories

I wanted to write to Lil and ask her to marry me, but I had no money to buy an engagement ring. Still in Ireland, at Drewstown House, I shared my prayer request with the staff and Mrs Kimmel, the warden's wife. Very soon afterwards, she appeared with both engagement and wedding rings. These had been given to her by her father, once a laundry owner in the US. He had found them when dry cleaning a suit but the suit owner had never returned to claim them. She handed the rings over to me saying, 'Now you can propose to Lilian'. I was speechless and very happy. Finally, I was able to write the long-awaited letter and ask the question, 'Will you marry me?'. The wonderful answer was 'Yes'. We were now engaged, sealing our promise by letter in May 1958. In October, I left for Austria, where Lil, the Schwaigmühle, ten children and a whole world of work awaited me.

The Renovation of the Schwaigmühle: Our Shared Memories

The Schwaigmühle, The Mill, was a farmhouse, more than 400 years old, in whose mill grain was processed for many years, and bread was baked and sold. In the course of buying the property, various rights were purchased. These included rights for fishing, farming and grazing, wood, water and gravel. All of these were vital for our future life, but particularly so, the gravel rights, as gravel was such an important building material. If all these rights had not been acquired, then they would have remained with the original owner of the Schwaigmühle. The building itself was uninhabitable and had to be completely renovated before we could think of moving in. Additional staff were urgently needed to get this major project underway.

Joe Coulson had good experience in building and had a clear picture in his mind of what our future house might look like. However, we were not sure that he realised the Schwaigmühle was built of stone! Nevertheless, he dragged buckets of material out of the house, alongside rotten floor beams. He planned a concrete floor, but, in those days, there was no ready-made material, so everything had to be mixed by hand. Even the small windows that were quite common then had to be enlarged. There were thousands of things to do, and we worked continuously. We had a 'system', whereby the men spent Monday to Saturday on the building work, along with one female who did the cooking and assisted where possible; and the children were looked after by the other women in St. Jakob. We all met up on Sundays for church and fellowship. There is so much more to say about the renovation of the Schwaigmühle, and that story will continue later. However, we step aside from the work in Austria for a brief time, as there was a wedding to plan back in England. Lil takes up the story…

Our Wedding

Rob had gone back to Ireland to collect his belongings, and I returned to London and my family. At Christmas 1958, Rob came to London, and a week later we got married. My 'home church family' from the Bermondsey Gospel Mission did a fantastic job in taking care of many of the wedding arrangements. This is the wonderful thing about a church family; they want to support and provide whatever they can. My mother and my friend Hilda were also such a great help in giving me an unforgettable day. Hilda had made a wedding dress for her sister-in-law, and she lent this to me. It was a perfect fit. My sisters, who were already married, also gave me other things I needed.

Meanwhile, Rob had acquired a wedding suit from his uncle. We still needed to find him some wedding shoes. There was a popular song at this time called 'Second Hand Rose', all about using old things. I remember thinking about those words when collecting all our clothing items for the wedding. The actual wedding day itself was 3 January 1959, an icy cold winter day, but the fire of love burned in our hearts. It was a truly wonderful celebration.

We are married, so from now on, we share joint memories

The Honeymoon

Where could you go on your honeymoon when you have hardly any money? Well, we borrowed a car from friends and drove to Hastings, a coastal resort on the south coast of England. We stayed at a guest house for Salvation Army workers. When the director of the guest house heard we were on honeymoon, he gave us a generous discount, and we paid £5 for our one-week stay. We remember fondly, our walks along the beach whilst watching the high waves of the English Channel. Once back in our room, we huddled together in front of the radiator to thaw out from the freezing cold temperatures outside.

After the honeymoon, we spent about eight weeks visiting churches in England and Scotland, giving talks about our work. Then in March 1959, it was time to return to Salzburg and continue the renovation of the Schwaigmühle.

The Challenges of Living and Renovating

Due to our work circumstances, we had to put our married life on the back burner for a short while. Rob energetically worked and 'camped' at The Mill all week, whilst the women were mostly looking after the children in St. Jakob. Gradually, the renovation progressed, but the building was not yet ready to house all of us, including the children. In the summer of 1959, we all lived at the Schwaigmühle. We slept on camp beds, and during the day the children played at the well or in the forest. They were happily occupied throughout the day while we all tried to finish more of the building work. The tenancy agreement on the house in St. Jakob was due to finish in November so we knew we would have to move out and live at the Schwaigmühle. It wasn't going to be easy as our home was nowhere near finished, but we had no choice. Within three days, without the help of professional house movers, we transported all our belongings, furniture and boxes from St. Jakob to Großgmain. The house windows had yet to be made, so the plastic ones had to suffice even though it was wintertime. We had wooden doors at the front and back of the house, neither of which could be locked. Inside there were no doors, so we fixed army blankets in each door frame which we got from the American soldiers, who were stationed in Germany. The building was heated with a kitchen woodstove and oil heater, whilst drinking water came from a small spring on the hill. In the house was a 'slide' on the first floor where the excrement had been carried out. Was this supposed to be a toilet? Rob didn't hesitate, tearing it down to improve the hygiene within the house. Soon a toilet was installed. Today, the authorities would have intervened but not so then. Rob blossomed as the building progressed, and the more of us in the house, the happier he was!

Joe continued to be our master builder, and the neighbours thought we were crazy, but it wasn't long before they began to renovate their farmhouses. Joe had inspired them and shown what was possible. Although we spoke a different language and had different beliefs to our neighbours, they really accepted us.

Whilst Joe and Rob continued the building work, Lil was fully occupied with language learning, childcare, cooking, cleaning and laundry. Washing laundry was a lengthy process which took many hours. Thanks to the American soldiers, we had a partially automatic electric washing machine, but the rest of the washing was done by hand. After washing, the laundry had to be physically turned through a mangle.

The Austrian Rain

The Austrian weather presented its own challenges with heavy rain often falling within a short space of time. On one occasion we had a group of English helpers, and some of us had driven out to a prayer meeting in the car. Whilst out, there had been heavy rain, and the stream had overflowed its banks and cut off our way back. We left the car and accessed the house via the pedestrian bridge and over the slope. We were grateful to be in the dry, but meanwhile the stream continued to swell, and our small wooden bridge was washed away. This had been our only connection to the road. Our English helpers were due to leave the following day, but without a bridge, they could not depart. These helpers decided to build a 'construction' to get over the stream. Large stones in rows were placed in the water with huge strong planks laid over them. One helper dared to drive over this construction.

Lee covered her eyes. Thankfully, it worked! We knew what our next urgent project had to be, and, as soon as there was time, Rob and Joe built a stable bridge with steel girders. Never again would our bridge be washed away by heavy rain. We were convinced that even a tank could drive over this wonderful construction.

The Renovation Goes On and On

Over the next few years, we gradually completed much of the remaining work in the house. We did not have to do this alone: from 1959 onwards, nine different work camps from across the world came and supported us. The Mennonites (a Christian organisation) enlisted students from Holland, Sweden, Germany, Canada and America, to come and work under Joe's leadership, until good progress had been made on the building. Together, they helped to lay drainage pipes, close holes, lay floors and, happily, they cooked for themselves. What a blessing! We even had an Egyptian and Indian amongst team members. They not only helped with the manual work but also enjoyed fun-time with the children. Some of the students spoke a little German, but most conversed in English. The children enjoyed having all these helpers around and picked up on some of their phrases, for example 'No kidding'. The children asked what this meant, and we couldn't help but translate 'No kids'. We also received support in the form of 'care packages' from the Mennonites, namely large amounts of chicken, turkey, pork, beef, cheese, dried milk, dried eggs, rice and flour. The latter was taken to the baker so bread could be made for us. We had acquaintances who owned a company and sent frequent donations of woollen clothing.

The older children attended the local school in Großgmain and were warmly welcomed by the headteacher. We drove them to the school in the morning, and they usually walked back, a distance of five kilometres. This walk took them at least an hour, often more. They enjoyed stopping off at several farms and looking at the animals. After homework, tea and Bible study, the children took a bath, firstly the girls and then the boys. Each day was very busy and with such a wide range of ages, it was not always easy to keep them occupied. The children helped out at home, by feeding the chickens and cleaning out the cow house. They learned what to do on a farm and in an extended family. They loved doing these jobs. At the weekends, Joe and Lee often went to Vienna to see family.

The Schwaigmühle was a place where lots of visitors were welcomed from a wide range of countries. Missionaries from Austria and beyond called by, as did US army soldiers, who on their days off would often go to nearby Berchtesgaden to ski or play golf. Sometimes, they made a detour to us, bringing presents for the children; for example, clothes, toys and sweets. We can remember the excitement in the children's eyes when this happened. Although we never quite imagined this kind of missionary service when at Bible College, we were very happy in this environment. Our motto has always been: 'Ready for everything.' It was a most interesting few years at the beginning of married life, living alongside others and not having that much time to ourselves. Soon, we noticed a big difference between our two cultures; 'the American will never endure something if it can be changed, whereas the English will never change if they can help it.' Well, that was our observation! Rob felt 'at home' anywhere, probably because as a child, his family had moved around so much. Lil, on the other hand, always needed a little more time to call a new place 'home'.

The Coulsons

As already mentioned, Joe was a gifted builder. Lee was also talented, good at sewing as well as cooking. She was not afraid of hard work and managed the children very well.

What a cheerful presence she was in the house and also highly regarded in the neighbourhood. She always dressed smartly and particularly enjoyed wearing Austrian national costume. Joe had taught her to drive, and her skills were much appreciated in that respect.

Lee's parents from Vienna were also a great help and came every week to support our work in very practical ways. 'Mr Seimann', as we called him, worked alongside Rob. Initially, Rob spoke little German and Mr Seimann no English, but somehow, they managed to understand each other. Occasionally, Lee was called over to explain things further. Mr Seimann, who became known as 'Grandpa', was a good man and hugely appreciated by Rob. His wife, known as 'Grandma', was also a real asset and loved the children very much. Since Joe and Lee had no biological children of their own, the orphan children were, in a sense, the grandchildren of the Seimanns. We also enjoyed the company of Aunt Resi, who sometimes came from Vienna.

Without a doubt, Joe was unmistakably talented in his position at the Schwaigmühle and a true pioneer. Again, and again, we had the impression that with God's help, he was given special wisdom that no one else in this situation would have had. He was great at making decisions, inspirational with ideas and quick at learning the German language with the help of his Austrian wife. He would hear a new word in German and could immediately pronounce and use it. He had a charismatic personality, which came in very useful when dealing with the public. On occasions, articles appeared in the newspaper about the children under such headlines as 'Uncle Joe's Cabin and Uncle Joe and his ten little negroes'. Of course, today, such choice of words in a newspaper would be unthinkable. We still have a portfolio of press cuttings about the children, which the Coulsons passed onto us. In June 2012, Joe and Lee received a 'Pro Caritate' merit badge from the province of Salzburg, for their work all those years ago. In a letter they included us in their appreciation saying, 'We were a team, we appreciated your willingness, loyalty and co-operation, a million thanks to Rob and Lil. This recognition is as much yours, as it is ours. We love you'.

1960–1961

During this time, The Mill renovation continued. The children flourished, all growing up with plenty of space to play, both in the house and outdoors. Hills, a stream, a forest, animals – they loved this environment.

In May 1960 Rob had appendicitis and underwent an operation. After discharge from the hospital, he was supposed to be taking a lot of rest, but he took the opportunity to build a large built-in wardrobe in our bedroom. This wonderful construction served us well for several decades.

In the autumn of 1960, we were asked by the World Missions to Children to go to Drewstown House in Ireland (a place we knew well!) to help in the home. There were staffing shortages, and we helped out for a few months. Sadly, whilst there, we heard that Fritzi, one of our young orphans, had died. He was only six years old but had experienced poor health from birth. In due course, we returned to Austria and shortly after that, Joe and Lee departed for their furlough in America.

Fortune in Misfortune: The Fire

We remember the date only too well. It was Tuesday, 6 February 1962, and the weather was cold and snowy. Lil had just recovered from a tonsil operation, Joe and Lee were in America, and we were keeping the Schwaigmühle running with friends and helpers. Rob had decided to get his truck driver's licence, so we both took the bus into Salzburg. Lil had various things to do in the city while Rob went to the driving school. An urgent phone call came from The Mill to the driving school for Rob's attention. We had to return home immediately as the Schwaigmühle was on fire. It would take us a while to get there; first the bus journey (about fifty mins), then the long walk uphill from the bus stop, about a kilometre. We were tired and anxious.

As we approached home, we could see the smoke and flames. We could hardly believe what was happening; we were in total shock. On arrival, we saw the fire brigade who had put their hoses into the stream to access water to quench the flames. Our six adult helpers who were in the house at the time, had brought out the children calmly and rescued the animals. The latter were put in a neighbouring barn. At first, we both felt desperate, but within a few minutes, we hastily tried to rescue some essential items from the house. More and more people gathered; neighbours, friends, farmers and strangers all helped out. Despite all our efforts, we lost a huge amount in the fire. Our wedding gifts, stored in the attic, along with the Coulsons possessions (they had put things in storage before they left), were all lost.

Once the fire had been put out, and the building had cooled down, we went inside and surveyed the full extent of the damage. The rooms, the staircase, the corridors were all hugely damaged. Much of what the fire itself did not destroy was destroyed by water and falling ashes. The roof was completely burnt, and in time, the men threw the beams to the ground. The farmers'[3] insurance provided support.

The fire was a huge tragedy for us, but no one was considered negligent as the exact cause of the blaze was never established. We were so grateful for the many helpers who not only supported us at the time but in the following days. Neighbours brought wooden slats to build a temporary roof, and within six weeks we had a totally new one. The women and children stayed with the neighbours for a short time, where they were welcomed and looked after so well. Rob and another staff member slept in the garage, close to the house, to guard our premises. Step by step, with God's help, we fought our way through the clean-up work. Whilst we were devastated that our beloved Schwaigmühle had burned down, some good things came out of this terrible adversity. In the end, the house was much enlarged, we could build three metres higher, and we had a splendid new roof.

It took from February 1962 until the summer of 1962 before our house resembled what it was before. We cleaned and cleaned, disposed of broken things and repaired many other objects. New floors were laid, the interior and exterior were painted white, and we now had central heating throughout the building. The latter was installed by an English plumber. Little by little, the Schwaigmühle became tidy and

---

[3] Farmers' insurance was a shared agreement between farmers in the whole county of Salzburg. If a disaster, e.g. a fire, happened on a particular property, local farmers supported the renovation work through the provision of materials, manpower and equipment. Farmers further afield would pay money towards the renovation.

beautiful again. A kind neighbour had noble relatives from Glanegg Castle and told the American consulate about our situation. We received many gifts, including new bunk beds for the children.

Joe Coulson came back from America briefly, to survey what had happened but then returned home. He and Lee only returned in late 1962. We had wonderful helpers during the rebuilding: three young Americans from the Mennonite church, two other men who had joined our Mission and also Edna Reading. We were hugely grateful for those who assisted us in this massive restoration. When this phase of the renovation was completed, we realised that out of this tragedy had come a new opportunity to serve God through our building. Without increased space in the house, new interiors and a high roof, the authorities would never have given permission for our youth camps in later years.

Chapter 4

Our First Homeward Journey
and its Consequences

But Jesus said, 'Go home to your own people and tell them how much the Lord has done for you'.

Mark 5 v 19

Adventure in America

Soon after the Coulsons returned late 1962, we left for our furlough and deputation work in the United States, going via London to see Lil's family. The Coulsons lent us money so we could buy a car for our trip. We purchased a VW Beetle, drove to London, and on 8 December 1962, we boarded the *Queen Mary*. Meanwhile, our 'Beetle' was transported by cargo ship. We were at sea for five days, and Lil experienced severe seasickness. Also, with loud music and dancing in the ship's dining room each evening, we had little sleep during our time on board. On arrival in New York, we collected our car and found that the spark plugs had been stolen! After repairs, we started our tour of America.

What is Furlough and Deputation Work?

For those readers unfamiliar with these terms, let us explain. The Mission expected their workers to travel back to their home country at regular intervals to meet with friends, family and church groups, to talk about their work. In doing this, the profile of the Schwaigmühle and our work would be raised, and hopefully, churches, and others, would begin or continue to support our work, through prayer and financial giving. Most of our meetings had to be planned well in advance, so months before departing from Austria, we had set up dates and times. Sometimes our programme had to be adapted, and more meetings were added to our schedule. Travel and accommodation also had to be pre-planned. It took a lot of organisation and, once 'on furlough', it was usually quite hectic and often tiring, involving lots of unpacking and then packing again, with constant changes of accommodation. In those days, there were no mobile phones or Internet, so communication was often problematic. Weather conditions, car problems, and varying travel times added complications. Even so, we visited lots of churches and supporters, gave talks and showed slides of our work. We were always welcomed, and listeners expressed much interest. Once back in Austria, we sent out regular prayer letters to our supporters. These furloughs sometimes lasted up to a year and at other times, just a few months.

Our Deputation Work Begins

Our first stop was New York, where we visited the sister of one of Rob's colleagues from his navy days. Her brother was considered 'lost' in the Korean war. Next, was an enjoyable visit to Bethany College in Minneapolis, followed by a day when miraculously God protected us from a serious accident after a trailer came loose from its vehicle, passing us on the highway. We always prayed for our travel, but after that, we did so even more. Our next destination was Rob's brother, JT, in Rapid City, South Dakota. Then, after nearly four years of marriage, Lil was to meet Rob's family. It was Christmas 1962, and we were in Cupertino, near San Francisco, California. We stayed there a month where Lil experienced 'Shopping Californian style' with Rob's mother. She delighted in telling her friends and neighbours about her new English daughter-in-law, inviting them to come and meet her. Many came to hear about our work at The Mill, in Großgmain. From there, we visited the Mission HQ in San Jose, took some rest, and got to know the people in the Maranatha church. It became like a spiritual home for us each time we visited Rob's parents in Cupertino.

Long Journeys

We travelled north and south on the west coast, and over to the Midwest, all the time being grateful for our reliable Beetle. Months later, we traded in our Beetle for an ancient Renault. It had a couple of holes in the floor and the windscreen wipers didn't work properly. Lil rescued the situation during a very windy and wet storm in Colorado, by operating them manually from the passenger seat. On another journey, from the state border of Nevada to Salt Lake City in Utah, we broke down as our car radiator got hot, boiled over, and we had no water to fill it up. We hailed down a truck driver who took us to a gas station where an attendant came to our rescue. He took us back to our car and filled up the radiator. He charged us ten dollars, one for the water and nine for his expertise! After that, we always kept a bottle of water handy for our leaking radiator!

We didn't just visit Christian communities, but also our families and friends. We depended on our supporters for regular financial donations. Christians may give to different causes, but we were always grateful when they contributed something, however small, to our work in Austria. Basically, we lived from day to day, relying on God to provide for all our needs, and He always did and still does. We, too, supported others in their Christian work.

Although our deputation work was busy and tiring, we enjoyed it. We gave many talks and experienced some amazing hospitality. One time when in Seattle, two ladies invited us to a very good restaurant to sample 'Smorgasbord' – one price enabled the diner to eat as much as they could manage. We left feeling very full. That evening we met up with some of Rob's friends from Bible School, and together with other couples, we found ourselves eating in a Smorgasbord restaurant again! Occasionally, between all the talks and travel, we had the opportunity for a little sightseeing, and there were some interesting conversations with strangers. Certainly, our deputation work was a total change from our everyday life in Austria, and some days it felt like a holiday.

We were due to complete our time in the US in November 1963, so on 22 November we were back in New York, ready to board the transatlantic ship, the *Mauretania*. As we stood on deck, waving goodbye to our friends, we heard the announcement that John F Kennedy had been shot. Even today, there are many people who can remember exactly where they were when they heard this news about the American president.

We had many more trips to America: 1968/69, 1974/75, 1980/81, 1984, 1987/88, 1993, 1999, and then our last trip in 2004, when we were aged seventy-five.

Positive Personal News

Back in London, we spent some time with Lil's family and friends. We did three months travelling and went as far as Scotland to talk about our work with orphans in Austria and receive support for our ministry. Lil underwent a small gynaecological operation to try and find out why she could not get pregnant. We had been married for several years and longed for a child. The doctors realised that a fallopian tube was not working and were able to rectify this situation. We were thankful and hopeful.

An Unexpected Letter

In March 1964, we received an official letter from the Mission leadership. It stated that the Coulsons had applied to adopt the orphan children and had received a court order to proceed. Their thinking was that it would be easier for the children to grow up in America, and emigration arrangements were already underway. We were to pack our bags and return to Austria to say goodbye to the children. We were in total shock on hearing this news. Why were we not privy to these plans? Had the plans moved more quickly than expected? What would this mean for our work at The Mill? We had just spent a year on deputation work, seeking prayer and financial support for orphan children in Austria, and now there were plans for these children to live in the US. We needed time to 'process' this news but began our journey back to Austria.

We boarded a train from London to Dover, then crossed the English Channel by boat, arriving in Ostend in Belgium. From there, it was a long journey back to Salzburg. On arrival at the Schwaigmühle, we had a few days with the children before they were collected by American soldiers and taken to the airport. The necessary legal and travel arrangements had been started by the Coulsons, but to their surprise, the plans moved very speedily. It seemed there had been a huge misunderstanding as to who would inform us of this news and exactly at what point in time. Being absent from Austria for over a year did make it slightly easier 'to let the children go'.

Joe and Lee tried to explain their motives to us, and we understood why it was best for the children to grow up in America. The older children would soon become teenagers, and living in Austria may not have provided good chances for their lives. We sensed the Coulsons had made the right decision, and even today, we believe it was the best thing for the children. However, the children had always called us aunt and uncle and had grown close to our hearts. They had now gone, and we were standing in a big, empty house. Joe had always been our boss, but who would take his place now? We felt very low in mood.

Chapter 5

Home in Austria: Change and Blessings

I will make them and the places surrounding my hill a blessing.
Ezekiel 34 v 26

April 1964, and we were settling back into life at the Schwaigmühle. The house was empty, the children had gone, along with our friends, the Coulsons. Both of us felt that God had placed us in Austria, and we wanted to continue here, but as yet, we had no plan. So much progress had been made on the renovation of the Schwaigmühle. We looked to God to 'open a new door' for us.

A New Plan for The Mill

Although the World Missions to Children had overall responsibility for the Schwaigmühle, it was our decision, jointly with the Mission, as to what we should do with the house. However, we had to agree a plan speedily; otherwise, the Mission would sell the house. The idea of a 'leisure home' seemed the way forward, but this term needs some explanation. Within a Christian context, this refers to a residential facility, where Christians can enjoy a holiday together, and at the same time receive Christian teaching. It entails a variety of activities, both indoors and outdoors: singing, drama, talks, discussion, walks, trips, etc. Perhaps the term 'Camp and Conference Centre' makes our idea clearer. We knew of such places across Europe and beyond, where families, young people or children, 'camped' during the summer and also at other times throughout the year. In our case, any 'campers' would reside indoors, with extra accommodation provided in tents in the grounds when needed.

This was now our plan for a new ministry as we believed The Mill was ideally situated in a beautiful location, with good facilities. In 1965, the Mission endorsed our proposal and permission was granted from the Salzburg authorities. This would enable us to welcome children and young people under eighteen. We had already done a very small trial in 1964, when an acquaintance from Vienna wondered how to occupy her sons during the long summer holidays. She needed to work but wanted her sons to be looked after safely and productively. Having heard about us, and after discussion, she sent her boys to The Mill. For six weeks we ran a programme for them, providing good food, and activities including some Bible teaching. We believed we could do the same with larger groups.

Helpers Needed!

Over time, Mr Baer, Vic Fedosky and our friend Edna Reading, our helpers over many years, had all left. We were now looking for new helpers. Fortunately, we knew of many churches and Christian organisations across Austria, including some in Salzburg. We got on well with all these groups. Not all shared the same theological perspective as ourselves, but we were clear that Jesus Christ would be at the centre of our ministry. We felt confident that God would provide the right helpers who shared our vision. We remembered the early missionary pioneers and believed God would provide for us, as he had for them. One of our earliest helpers was Berenice Jackson, then a young nurse from Australia. She first came in 1964 and returned again and again. There were also many other faithful friend-helpers.

God Blesses

Lil became pregnant in 1965 and, due to her medical history, it made sense for the baby to be born in London with her family to support her. The doctor in Salzburg agreed with this decision, since he thought there was a chance it might be a caesarean birth, and plenty of rest would be needed afterwards. In September, Lil travelled back to London with friends. Once the baby was born, Rob would travel to England. We had helpers who would look after the Schwaigmühle during our absence. On 24 November 1965, after a long, natural labour, our beautiful daughter, Elizabeth Anne, was born. Her name was a tribute to Queen Elizabeth II and also to the mother of John the Baptist. Lil's mother rang Austria to let Rob know the news, but he was out at a prayer meeting! He had to wait until the following morning before he heard that he had become a father. Both our families were overjoyed. Whilst Lil was desperate for Rob to join her, he had to sort out things on the domestic front before departing for London.

After discharge from hospital, Lil lived in a small flat with her mother, sister and family. There wasn't much space, but she was given the best room, and no one complained when baby Elizabeth cried a lot. Rob arrived in December when Elizabeth was three weeks old. From that moment on, father and daughter were inseparable.

Time to Return to Austria

In cold and wintry conditions, we loaded up the VW bus and tried to make our trip as comfortable as possible with a six-week-old baby. Thankfully, we had the help of Berry, the experienced nurse and midwife, who had been in London and travelled with us. In total, we were on the road for three days, staying overnight in Belgium with missionaries and in Stuttgart with friends. Our final moments of the journey were the most exciting when we had to cross the border from Bad Reichenhall into Großgmain. There was a dreaded, very strict border official, who enjoyed keeping cars waiting, then demanded that all items were unloaded to be checked meticulously. Naturally, we were anxious that he might be on duty. In those days everything had to be declared, and customs duty was payable on anything other than presents brought into Austria. On this occasion, the particular official was indeed on duty, and we prepared ourselves for the worst. He opened the car door, and the cold air entered. He saw a tiny baby in her travel cot, closed the door and waved us through. We had nothing to declare anyway but were so relieved that we had not been delayed. Within a few more minutes we were back at The Mill and were now a family of three. Once home, Elizabeth was lovingly welcomed into the community. We felt blessed.

The 'Camps' Begin

In the summer of 1965, we launched our first children and teenage camps. With huge energy and determination, we tried to do everything: organise the Christian teaching programme, plan outings, suggest activities, provide all meals and snacks, clean the house, tend the garden, do all the shopping, keep up with the bookkeeping and much, much more. As soon as one camp finished, a vast clean took place, and the whole cycle started again. It was not long before we realised that all this work, plus looking after a baby, was far too much for two people with only a few helpers coming and going. So, after much consideration, we decided to adapt our style to the local customs. From then on, the groups would book into The Mill, but they would take responsibility for the organisation of their programme. We would take care of everything else ensuring good accommodation and tasty food. However, we acted like 'house parents', and if leaders or children/young people needed support or help, we would listen and advise. Sometimes we would have a brief chat with a child on the stairs or outside, and one day some children were rather tearful. When Rob asked if they were feeling all right, one replied they had just been listening to the moving story of the death of Jesus and, having not heard it before, found it quite emotional. We were grateful for gifted camp leaders who could explain gospel stories and truths to children and young people. We enjoyed wonderful co-operation with lots of leaders and their teams over very many years.

Although we were now concentrating on running the house, and not the detail of the camp programme, life was still hugely busy. Throughout the summer, we had continuous weekly camps, each with about thirty children, without a day's rest. On the change-over day, one camp left in the morning and soon after lunch, the next campers arrived. You can imagine the cleaning, sorting and shopping we had to do within a few hours. In autumn, winter and spring, the groups usually came Friday to Sunday. That was still a lot of work, although we had some breathing space during the week to catch up on all the jobs, some of which were ongoing. Upkeep of the house facilities could only be carried out when fewer people were around.

We had a large network of contacts within churches, not just in Austria but also in England and America. These 'contacts' were also useful for finding helpers. In some instances, large church groups came to spend their holiday at the Schwaigmühle. Großgmain is centrally located in Europe, so we were also able to meet and accommodate many passing missionaries on their way to the former Eastern Bloc. It was wonderful to share fellowship with these men and women who often encountered risky situations in the Lord's service.

Cheapy Deluxe Hotel and Friends for Life

We got ourselves a reputation for always providing a welcome, a warm bed and good food. And of course, a good cup of English tea! Anyone coming from England was under strict instructions to bring as many teabags as they could carry. Our Visitors' Book lists vast numbers of people who visited over many years. As much as we would like to mention them all, there are too many, so you will only hear about a few. A considerable number have remained good friends over so many years, and we are thankful.

Peter Torskyj had an English mother and Austrian father and was in Austria doing his military service (this is a mandatory requirement in Austria). He was not a Christian, but through a paramedic friend, Karl Fröhlich, he found faith. He later became the pastor at the Baptist church in Bad Ischl. His girlfriend at the time, and later his wife, Alide, worked with us during our camp season.

Len and Sylvia Muggeridge, known affectionately as 'the Muggs', had met in Austria. Len was a missionary here, and we first got to know him in 1959. He then met Sylvia, who was working in the Christian bookshop in Graz. Sylvia had some knowledge of Graz, as her father had been stationed there as a soldier some twenty years earlier. In 1966, Len and Sylvia spent their honeymoon with us at The Mill! They visited and helped us several times, including when they had four young children. Len assisted Rob in the house and garden while Sylvia helped in the house. Their cheerfulness and humour were such a blessing to us. When visiting England, they lent us their car and looked after us very well.

Sadly, Sylvia died of colorectal cancer in 1986, at the age of forty-four. This loss hit us very hard. We kept in touch with Len until he died in 2017, age eighty-eight and we now hear from Katie, their eldest daughter, who faithfully practises her Christian faith.

Another special couple were Herb and Lorelei Apel who were missionaries in Austria. Our friendship began when we first met them in Vienna, at a missionary conference, and stayed with them in their home. They often called by at The Mill; for example, one morning at 7a.m. when they were travelling to collect their children from boarding school in Lörrach, in Germany. They coined the phrase 'Cheapy, cheapy deluxe hotel' when referring to The Mill. Our principle was never to charge missionaries for accommodation when visiting us. The Apels were musical and sang 'O Sole Mio', a short operatic song, which became a Mill favourite. Making our own entertainment was a strong feature of Mill life. The Apels often joined us for our Easter missionary conference, which was also a holiday time.

Another great friend and helper was Hanns-Jörg Theuer, with whom we still have contact. During the late 1960s, he was very active in the Volksmission in Salzburg and was responsible for youth work in his church. He was strategic in helping us to set up The Mill Trust which, for legal reasons, we were asked to do. We recall with thanks and humour our meetings which Hanns-Jörg chaired, alongside a lawyer from the Mennonite community. Hanns-Jörg was meticulously efficient in recording the details of these meetings. He regularly visited the Schwaigmühle, bringing children and teenagers for recreational activities or quiet days.

We must also mention another 'connection' Hanns-Jörg had with The Mill. Hanns-Jörg's brother-in-law, Emanuel, proposed to Renate on the steep meadow next to The Mill. Yes, there were many sweet, romantic moments, proposals of marriage, and even wedding receptions on the meadow in front of the Schwaigmühle.

These were good days, and we felt very blessed.

Elizabeth Thrives and Excels Living the Schwaigmühle Life

As a family, we were always a team. Lil was fully occupied with cooking and cleaning for the camps with hardly a minute's break. Rob took Elizabeth everywhere he went, watching over her twenty-four hours a day. She had to be supervised, but he was never impatient with her as he went about his many tasks, with Elizabeth in tow. At night, Rob was the one to get up if he was needed, changing nappies and rocking our daughter back to sleep.

Even in her early months and years, Elizabeth wanted to be 'on the go'. She stood up at six months and started walking at nine and a half months. At four, she attended Kindergarten and was a very sociable child. However, there were linguistic challenges for her since at home we always spoke English, whilst at Kindergarten, she was surrounded by German speakers. Rob was the first Kindergarten bus driver, collecting neighbours' children on the way.

Elizabeth was an only child, but from an early age, she related well to anyone who came into the house. When she was very young, we welcomed Wolfgang into our home. He was fourteen years old, had come into conflict with the law and felt like an outsider in his own family. He needed a foster family to be there for him. Together we formed a good relationship, and he lived with us for three years. He did well, getting an apprenticeship, completing his military service and later getting married. In retirement he moved to Hungary, and we are thrilled to still be in contact with him today.

We were always thankful to God for giving us a child, but we longed for another to complete our family. It was not to be, and in spring 1970, Lil had a miscarriage. It is still a comfort to know that one day, we will see our child in heaven. This event was a painful experience and much rest was needed. We had a quiet time at home in the weeks before the camps started.

As Elizabeth grew up, she enjoyed joining in with the campers and their many activities. Off she went with groups to swim, walk, play sports, take part in quizzes and Bible talks. Sometimes, she slept in a room with the campers in preference to her own bedroom!

Many Campers From Many Places

Our camp groups came from a variety of countries, for example, Austria, England, Germany and even Cambodia. The latter were refugees, living in Linz, and they certainly brought a whole new atmosphere to The Mill. They cooked noodles for breakfast and were not used to big spaces, so they appreciated The Mill with its large grounds. Our campers were children, young people, family groups, church groups with many coming back year after year. Actually, the camps of the adults did not look much different from those of the children: Bible teaching, excursions, fun activities, campfires, barbeques, and always a special last evening celebration finale. For this, everyone was invited to make a contribution, and some of the shows were legendary. Our life was never boring.

We also had 'work camps' such as in 1975 when Teen Missions sent a group of older teenagers to transform our old hayloft into a conference room. Together with experienced leaders, they installed windows, sealed the walls and made an excellent start in creating this new facility.

When we had English-speaking visitors in the house, Elizabeth spent a lot of time with them. Accompanying them on their trips to all the key tourist sites, she explained the history and translated as necessary. She was an expert on where to buy the best Austrian souvenirs and would speak to the shopkeepers re pricing. *Sound of Music* tours were also a firm favourite of our English guests, so again Elizabeth would tell the story of the musical and point out the different locations, suggesting the best photo opportunities.

Throughout the camp season, we had helpers from several different countries. Extensive help was needed with the cooking and cleaning and Lil 'trained up' people all the time. You cannot assume that everyone knows how to clean properly and efficiently, so Lil provided the guidance. Rob had helpers too, and again he directed as needed. It was always great when helpers returned because they already 'knew the system'. If we were ever short of helpers, then we just had to manage somehow. Once, when Lil was unwell in bed, and there were no helpers available, Elizabeth found herself in charge. She cleaned toilets, washed the floors and took over the kitchen. Very successfully, she managed to cook goulash for about forty guests with the occasional question to Lil upstairs, in bed with a fever.

You may be wondering what it was like to be a worker at The Mill during 'camp time'. There was never, ever a typical day, but the pattern outlined below perhaps gives you a kind of picture.

Our Daily Schedule During Camps

5.00: Rob gets up and makes an early morning cup of tea for Lil and himself. If requested, Rob also delivers cups of tea to any helpers.

6.30: Lil, in the kitchen, prepares breakfast for campers. Rob does jobs inside/outside the house, and drives to the bakers in Großgmain to collect fresh rolls for breakfast.

7.00: Family and helpers have breakfast, followed by Bible reading and prayer.

8.00: Campers' breakfast; fresh rolls, butter and jam on tables, cocoa in pots and bread sliced.

8.30-8.45: Couple of campers do their breakfast washing-up (no dishwasher in those days).

9.00: Campers to their morning meeting.

9.00: Cleaning starts. The 'cleaning helper' sweeps all public rooms, washes floors, cleans toilets and bathrooms. Washing into the machine, put outside to dry. Helper assists Lil with lunch preparation (always a substantial cooked meal with pudding).

Meanwhile, Rob (and any helpers), does endless jobs in the house, and outside, goes shopping and much more, e.g. mowing the grass around The Mill with the bulky manual lawnmower.

12.00:   Campers eat lunch whilst family and helpers try to eat theirs, but often have interruptions from camp leaders for more food, juice, or questions.

13.00:   Campers do their washing-up, and Lil cleans the kitchen. *Jause* (afternoon snack of bread or cake) prepared. The house is generally quiet for an hour.

14.00:   Campers go outside for activity/walks/visits. Rob and Lil and helpers attempt a short rest.

15.00:   *Jause* is served for campers, after which they return to activities, e.g. walk, outings. Meanwhile, Lil and helper start preparing tea.

18.00:   Tea for campers. Usually bread with cheese, cold meats and gherkins. Meanwhile, family and helpers eat tea. Afterwards, washing and tidying up. The dining room is then set up for breakfast.

Weekly campfire is usually on the last night of camp, eating potato salad and sausages, marshmallows and lots of good brown bread.

19.00:   Campers attend the evening meeting, then usually in their bedrooms by 21.30.

Family and helpers enjoy their evening. Sometimes there are visitors; at other times they make their own entertainment. Often games are played, for example, Null, a Schwaigmühle favourite, or Pit. Occasionally, there is so much noise that even the camp leaders kindly asked the residents to be a little quieter! Early bedtime unless Rob decides to make popcorn or serve ice cream.

One of the special features of our camps was 'Rob's sweetshop' where some heavenly sweets could be bought cheaply. This was so appreciated by the children's camps. Then there was also our unique ice cream machine brought back from our travels. Making the ice cream was a huge effort, with the ice having to be made first. We decided to 'bypass' this, and bought ice from a nearby brewery, hammering it into smaller pieces and putting it into cartons, and finally into the machine. Our guests were delighted, but Rob was not satisfied with the quality of the product as it tasted rather like frozen yogurt. For his ninetieth birthday, we gave him a proper ice cream maker, and this machine delivered on quality. Ice cream has always remained his favourite sweet dish, enjoyed whatever the season of the year.

There were always ongoing renovation projects at the Schwaigmühle, and in 1974 we got our own personal living area, a small three-room apartment on the top floor. This was an awaited day of absolute joy.

It was difficult to plan deputation work in America and England since there were always camps booked. Even during autumn and winter there were weekend camps so we couldn't leave unless we found a couple, or a group of people who could take over the house, camps and the many jobs while we were away. It wasn't easy finding the right people. Also, we didn't want to take Elizabeth out of school too much, though when we did in 1974/75, we operated 'home schooling' as we travelled. It was highly successful, and we recall Elizabeth advancing in her mathematical studies so much so, that when she returned to school, she was on page seventy-five of the textbook and her classmates were on page twenty-five! She learned easily and well and gained much from our travels.

Our daughter became a very confident traveller from an early age. With all her relatives in America and England, she was keen to visit and meet as many as possible. At the age of eleven, she flew alone to England to visit her grandmother, and when she was fourteen, and we were all travelling together, she had to return early, due to school commitments. Even though she was accompanied by her friend Wendy, we were still nervous about this journey. Fortunately, Elizabeth did not sense our anxiety and has wonderful memories of this journey.

Romance

When Elizabeth was fifteen years old, she was baptised, and not long afterwards, a lovely young man came into her life. This was Georg, and we liked him straight away. We noticed that we started to take 'more of a back seat' in Elizabeth's life as Georg became more central to hers! Happily, we watched the two of them get to know each other better, and Georg found faith in the Lord Jesus. We now know that Georg proposed to Elizabeth secretly in August 1982, but it was only when Elizabeth turned eighteen that they told us their plans.

Elizabeth and Georg's Wedding

This was planned for 2 August 1986, and so we began to think as to how we would finance the occasion. Our budget was very limited, so it was clear that this would be a small and modest wedding. But then, a miracle happened, and we felt blessed again. A lady in Los Angeles had decreed that after her death, the proceeds of her house should be distributed among several missionaries. We were given $1,000 for personal use. That was a lot of money in those days and, with 18,000 schillings (pre-euros) we felt a beautiful celebration could be arranged. The reception would take place at the Schwaigmühle, and we invited lots of people. Not only were there family and friends from Austria, but also America and England. A chef friend and his wife, Wendy, organised the catering. It was a dream wedding.

Another Miracle

Over the years, there was never a surplus of money, but we had confidence that God would provide as our needs arose. Whilst on deputation and telling people about our work, their donations would go directly to the Mission. This way, they could get a receipt, and deduct a small sum of money from their taxes. Some donations were given to us directly, for private use, and we used this money for our daily needs. However, there were times when we felt close to despair. Such was the case when, one day, a letter came from the Austrian authorities asking us to pay taxes retrospectively for a number of years. In a complicated tax system for missionaries, there had been confusion over when we should pay, and how much. However, with God's help, we got through this challenging time.

Unrelated to the tax issue just mentioned, sometime later, we were blessed to receive a huge donation from an English builder, known to some friends of ours, who had put a large surplus of the money he had earned into a trust. This money somehow found its way to us for the upkeep of The Mill and any future small building projects. Yet again, we felt very blessed. Sometime after that, we looked for a tax consultant in Salzburg to advise us on financial matters and later discovered that this dear lady was, and still is, a strongly religious woman. Another blessing!

In our Christian lives, we have experienced many challenges, but also many 'miracles', large and small, and can testify that God has always provided for our needs.

Rob and family

Lil with siblings

Rob in naval suitcoat

Lil at Redcliffe College

Drooping the colour

Lil with David

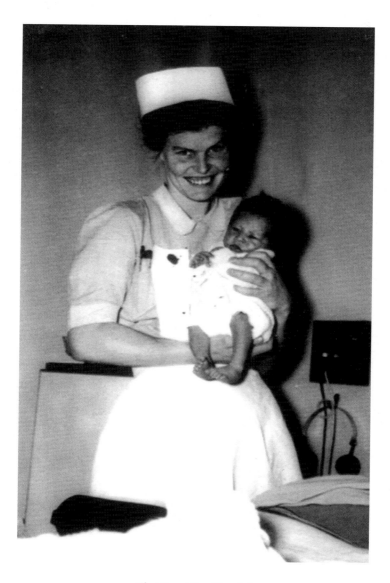

Lil at Royal Free Hospital

Tapeley Park House

Drewstown House Ireland

Lil and Lee with the orphans at St Jakob

The Mill when purchased in 1958

Rob renovates

Renovation work

Rob and Lil looking 'Austrian' 1958

Rob and Lil's wedding London 1959

Lil doing laundry outside 1960

The orphans with Schunnemans, Coulsons and other helpers

Renovation work

Rob the farmer

Fire at the Mill

Rob's Kindergarten bus

Rob, Lil & Elizabeth plus Schufti & Asher

Joe & Lee Coulson with Pro Caritate Award

The renovated Mill 1970

Lil & Rob's 90th Party Oct 2019

Chapter 6

Goodbye to the Schwaigmühle

The Years Go By

We have a guest book that captures the years 1964–1987. These are the years in which we managed the Schwaigmühle as a camp and conference centre, a Christian leisure home. We did some counting and discovered people visited us from across twenty different countries and thirty different states of America. We remember especially the Teen Missions who came with young volunteers from nine states. There were other volunteers too, who expanded the rooms on the second floor. We were very grateful for all this help.

1987–1988

In 1987, we went back to America for a year to do deputation work. In our absence a family took over the running and organisation of The Mill. Two months into our travels, December 1987, we visited the World Missions to Children headquarters in Grants Pass, Oregon, and met with the director. He informed us that the Mission believed The Mill now needed different structures and a new direction. This meant that we were not able to continue our work at the Schwaigmühle.

We were hugely disappointed and shocked, but we respected the decision of the leadership of our Mission. After much discussion and prayer, we resigned from the Mission. It was now early 1988, and since we had worked with them for so very many years, there were lots of issues that needed to be sorted. This took many months, but once we were back in Austria, we left The Mill. We felt hurt as it seemed there was another, and a possibly better way of running The Mill, that would prove more advantageous. We had put all our energy into this house, first for the orphans and then later for our guests and campers, in the context of a Christian centre.

God Knows Best

We thought about the Mission's decision and accepted that God wanted the best for us. On reflection, we came to realise that God was taking a real burden off our shoulders and was releasing us to do other things. We felt like a farmer, having sown seeds, tended the fields and watched the harvest grow, but then just before the final harvest, a hailstorm had come and ruined everything. However, we took stock: 'Lord, we have done our work in your name and whatever you have planned for us now, is in your purposes.' We realised that our work at the Schwaigmühle had been successful. It was a place of blessing for many individuals and groups from many nations. We know this because so many people told us. As long as the building stands and people are willing to work for it, God will continue to bless.

Although the Mission felt it would be a good idea for us to leave the locality and work elsewhere, we felt our life belonged in Großgmain, our local village, and we wanted to remain in this area which we knew well. Some dear friends of ours, who ran a missionary work in Großgmain, gave us some of their accommodation to rent until we found our own apartment. Simultaneously, our then pastor of the Baptist church in Salzburg, Graham Lange, offered us an opportunity to work in some areas of church life. Since we still received personal financial gifts from various supporters, we were able to serve the congregation free of charge.

An Unexpected Visit

Meanwhile, the Schwaigmühle continued to remain empty from March to September 1991, following the departure of the last workers. There had been no contact with the Mission during this time, but then one day something happened. The director of the Mission and a member of the board, without our knowledge, travelled to Großgmain to take a look at The Mill. They were keen to locate 'the Schunnemans', knowing we had stayed in the area but having no idea where we were now living. They went to the police station in Großgmain and asked for information on our whereabouts and were then able to locate our apartment. We knew that a neighbour of the Schwaigmühle had a key, so we accompanied the two men to The Mill. On arrival, it was a sad sight. Inside, the walls had turned green, the air was damp, and mould was growing everywhere. We made a fire, and although the two men had hoped to stay there, it was clearly impossible.

Immediately, we suggested they stayed with us in our apartment where there was a small spare room for guests. Almost a little ashamed, the director asked us to forgive him and the Mission for the unfortunate way they had dealt with our situation. The Mission was sincerely sorry. They began to realise just how much of our lives we had 'given' to The Mill and in so doing had built up an effective place for Christian ministry. We accepted the apology and supported the Mission in the restoration of the Schwaigmühle that we had left four years earlier. No one knew the workings of the house like Rob, so his help and advice proved invaluable. This was gratefully accepted, but for us, our time at The Mill was over, and to return was not an option.

As we looked back at the history of The Mill, there had been several changes. To begin with, the building was in the name of Joe Coulson for the land register before it became the property of the Mission in 1972. About that time too, the WMC changed its name to become the World Missions Fellowship, since their focus was no longer primarily supporting orphan children. In 2001 the Mission was dissolved and The Mill was sold to an Austrian association.

The Schwaigmühle has New Life Again

In September 1991, a new family arrived at The Mill and started restoration work in an attempt to bring this house back to its former glory. There was some damage in the conference room as pipes had frozen. The house was largely uninhabitable, and Rob went over regularly to help with woodwork and related house matters. Rob assisted a young man in the forest to secure wood for the house. The two men enjoyed working together very much. After ten years, the family left the Schwaigmühle.

In the following years, several couples led the work, and today the Schwaigmühle continues to function as a Christian centre but is self-catering. Groups either have to cook their own meals or employ their own cooks. Eventually new house parents took over. (Current details of The Mill can be found on their website. See Appendix 6.)

'Shall I Take Her to my Place?'

In 1997, Lil was admitted to hospital with severe stomach pains. The suspicion of intestinal obstruction was quickly confirmed, and emergency surgery was performed. It was such a difficult and emotional time for Rob as he sat in our Großgmain apartment. He heard God speaking to him about Lil's condition. Was now the time that God would 'take' Lil to heaven? Rob, deep with emotion, told God honestly how he was feeling; 'Lord, whatever you have prepared for me, I will take from your hand.' Rob knew that if Lil died, somehow God would provide the strength he needed to carry on without her. She would always be his beloved wife.

Wonderfully, the Lord gave grace, and Lil survived the operation, remaining in hospital for seven weeks. It was a time of challenge for us all. Elizabeth, our daughter, and her family, lived near Graz, quite a distance away by car, but she came over regularly and stayed for long periods of time until Lil was strong enough to go to the rehab centre. At this time, Elizabeth had two young children, so they had to come over too, but God provided in this situation. The Kindergarten, which Elizabeth had attended as a child, was next door to our apartment. She was able to leave her children there for the morning while she assisted us in whatever way was necessary.

New Opportunities Open Up

After Lil's recovery we continued our ministry in the Baptist church. However, we were getting older, and needed more help. As time went on, Elizabeth and Georg's family grew, with four children of their own, plus various foster children. Lil started travelling to Stainz at regular intervals to help with the family. It became clear that if we did not relocate to be nearer family soon, then such a move would become even more difficult in later years. So, in 2001 we moved to Stainz. Of course, saying goodbye to the church congregation in Salzburg was difficult. They were like a family to us. We were also moving from an area we loved deeply. All those years at the Schwaigmühle, first, looking after the orphans, followed by our extensive ministry of camps and conferences. We left it all behind, but it remains in our memory every day – our work for God and our legacy.

But we looked into the future with a smile. We knew there would be many new, exciting tasks in store for us as we moved closer to our family. In and around the Koidl house, there would always be jobs to do, and we could help. It was a joy to see everyone growing up.

Once we got established in Stainz, we then began to join the church in the Falkenhofgasse in Graz. We took on some small ministries amongst the congregation there and have made some deep friendships. Meanwhile, we are getting older, and our grandchildren are developing into wonderful young people. We now have three great-grandchildren.

We look back on a rich and fulfilled life.

Chapter 7

A Final Reflection and Thanks

Then Samuel took a stone and set it up between Mizpah and Shen. He named it Ebenezer[4], saying, 'Thus far the Lord has helped us'.

1 Samuel 7 v 12

Looking back on our lives, we can but agree with these seven words of Samuel: 'Thus far the Lord has helped us.'

Without the help of God, we would not have experienced all the things of which we have spoken and written. From the beginning, first as individuals, and then together, we served God in Austria, our place of mission. It was our faithful God and Lord, our beloved Saviour Jesus Christ who empowered us, placed us in His service and carried us through. He gave us co-workers, friends, and helpers so that we could move forwards with confidence. But above all, God gave us each other. We were in the Lord's service as a married couple,

---

[4] *Ebenezer means 'stone of help'.*

which was such a great blessing. There were ups and downs, victories and defeats, growth and stagnation. But the Lord has always helped us. Until old age, the Lord has helped us. We look back and marvel at the faithfulness of God.

Note and Thanks From Lilian

Rob died in January 2020 and went home to be with his Lord and Saviour. This was his final goal to meet his Lord face to face in eternity.

A few days before his death, he mysteriously asked me for some money. It was only at his memorial service that I learned what he had organised: he had arranged for a tree to be planted in Jerusalem in Elizabeth and Georg's name. Along with all his memories which have found their way into this book and which reveal his loving nature to us, this little tree is his legacy. It reminds us of The Tree of Life and what God has prepared for us if we trust Him. It recalls His promise:

Yes, I am coming soon.

Revelation 22 v 20

To Family

A big thank you to all the generations in our family: our daughter, Elizabeth, her husband, Georg, our grandchildren and great-grandchildren. We would like to bless you Anne and Maurits, Simon, Thomas and Andrea, Jonathan and

Sabrina, Larissa, Anina, and Verena. May God encourage you all to stay close to the Lord no matter what may come. We dedicate this book to you and love each one of you very much.

To Others

Over the years, our family and many friends had suggested there should be a written record of our life stories. We had documents, artefacts and photos in abundance to aid this task. Four generations of our family had seen and stayed at The Mill during 2019, so even the very youngest family members knew where we had once lived and worked for so long. The time was now right to tell our story and create a book. But who would write this?

Someone was needed who knew The Mill well and who had the relevant skills and drive to make this happen. Isobel Vale in England, took on this task, having first been to the Schwaigmühle in 1969, and returned again and again. Huge thanks to Isobel and also Dave and Laraine Cook, also friends from England, who have supported this project.

Chapter 8

Postscript

2019 was a wonderful year of celebrations for Lilian and Robert Schunneman.

In January, they celebrated sixty years of marriage. Together with their family, they travelled back to a snowy Salzburg, stayed at The Mill, their home for twenty-nine years, and enjoyed a Thanksgiving Service at Salzburg Baptist Church. In total, they had lived in the Salzburg area for forty-three years. Many local friends gathered, alongside some visitors from England.

Then, in May, Thomas, one of their grandsons, married Andrea, at a big celebration at the church in Graz. Again, a delightful mix of Austrian and English friends and relatives made this such a special day.

In late October, Rob and Lil celebrated again, this time with a joint ninetieth birthday party.

I was present for all these wonderful occasions and witnessed their enjoyment and most importantly, their gratitude to God.

Then, as 2020 began, Rob became quite frail, and as Lil has mentioned, he died in January. It was a peaceful death, in his bedroom at the Koidl's house where he had been cared for so beautifully in his latter days. A Thanksgiving Service took place locally, and the plan was to hold another service in Salzburg in April.

I had planned to be there too, extending my stay, so that together with Lil, I could work on this book which had only just been started at a distance. Then Covid-19 began to spread across the world, and travel plans were halted. This book came into being over Zooms, emails, Word documents, providing access to family archives, writings and photographs. Thanks to God for the wonders of technology! In particular, I am grateful to Elizabeth Koidl for her permission to use and adapt parts of an unpublished manuscript and acknowledge the significant work of Carina Manutscheri and Bernadette Weiser.

'Robert und Lilian Schunneman – unser reiches Leben. Die Entstehung der Schwaigmühle – unser Lebenswerk.'

After Rob's death, Lil adjusted quickly and remained her usual disciplined self. She meticulously checked the book manuscript and happily and readily agreed to my additional material, including the appendices. She always welcomed my suggestions and ideas. With the help of Elizabeth, who ensured her mum had all the documents ready for Zooms, we three managed to make progress in our regular digital chats. In fact, Lil totally embraced this technology and rather enjoyed it!

Then, just a week after the final draft had been completed, the message came that Lil had suffered a massive stroke.

Elizabeth stayed with her in the hospital, and then she was brought home to their house. There, in the very same bedroom where her beloved Rob had died just six months earlier, Lil died peacefully in July.

How very wonderful that we were able to complete this manuscript just in time before Lil went to meet her Lord and Saviour.

The ashes of both Rob and Lil were buried at the same time, in the forest close by to their beloved Schwaigmühle.

My thanks to Elizabeth for her patience, encouragement, humour and technological skills as I inundated her with emails, documents and many requests relating to the book. Thanks also to Georg, who ensured the Zoom meetings were operating simultaneously in two Austrian households. Special thanks too, go to John Christopher and Hannah Christopher, for sketches and photos. They are from London and distant cousins from Lil's side of the family. Huge thanks also, to my friends Dave and Laraine Cook, careful proofreaders and great encouragers.

Finally, on a personal note, I have been very blessed by having known Rob and Lil Schunneman for over fifty years. Some readers will have known them too. Others have now 'met' them through this book. Whatever your situation, I pray that their story will 'stay' with you for some time and that you will feel blessed, encouraged and challenged by their faith and trust in God.

Isobel Vale

Robert Schunneman 1929–2020

Lilian Schunneman 1929–2020

Because of the Lord's great love, we are not consumed, for his compassions never fail. They are new every morning; great is your faithfulness.

Lamentations 3 vs 22, 23

Appendix I

Sketch Showing Location of The Mill

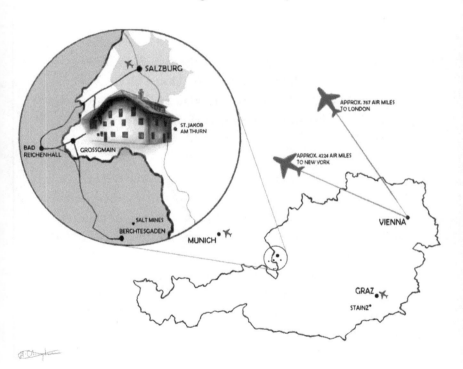

Appendix 2

Memories of the Schwaigmühle

Hundreds of people visited the Schwaigmühle in Austria. Below, just a few share their key memories of that place and also of Robert and Lilian Schunneman, who worked there between 1958–1987.

I visited The Mill twice. In 1962, all the children were there: Rob was busy putting in wooden floors in the bedrooms and porcelain in the bathrooms upstairs. The older children built a dam across the stream, so it was possible to swim. In 1973, I went to help, working in the kitchen and cleaning. It was very hard work. Lilly was a rock and led from the front. We had many memorable trips, including the salt mines. I hold very happy memories of a wonderful place and glorious enterprise.

Angela Staplehurst, Family Member/Helper
(Stoke-on-Trent, England)

I was placed in the orphanage a month after my twin brother and I were born. Our mother left us at the hospital, knowing she didn't have the strength or resources to raise us. For most of the first ten years of my life, I lived at The Mill. In 2014, I returned to Austria with my wife, Debbie. I have been so blessed by the positive influences so many people had on my life. They showed us God's unconditional love with practical guidance. They guided us by their Christlike example rather than the opinions of society. Thank you, Uncle Bob and Aunt Lilian, for the impact you had on my life.

Peter Hladec-Coulson, Orphan
(Boise, Idaho, US)

I remember Bob and Lil very well. They were part of my life when I lived at The Mill. As a child I had always known they loved the Lord. In 2016 I visited Austria and saw the Schunnemans. I will always remember the love they bestowed on all of us kids.

Gertie Fichtl Coulson-Lott, Orphan
(Beaverton, Oregon, US)

In 1984, I was on a six months' mission trip to Austria, staying at the Haus Rosenhof in Großgmain. I got to know Lil, Bob, Elizabeth and Georg at The Mill, who all welcomed me into their lives with open arms. I have so many good memories. Thank you for your love and acceptance and including me in so many things.

Tom Hoff, Visitor/Friend
(Napa, California, US)

I first met Rob and Lil in 1972, shortly after arriving in Salzburg to work as a nurse in the hospital. At that time, I didn't know anyone, and I couldn't speak German. Rob and Lil became my true brother and sister, welcomed me into their home, and The Mill became my second home. I have been, as many others, exceedingly blessed in knowing them.

Chrissie Prentice, Friend
(Salzburg, Austria)

In 1959, I had just left senior school, and our family drove to Austria to visit 'Auntie Lil' and 'Uncle Bob'. Once there, I helped with the orphan children but the highlights were going to work at the then derelict 'Mill'. I spent many hours soaking bricks for the chimney stack which was being built. Over the years we made return trips to enjoy the fun and loving friendship of the Schunnemans.

Shiela Stone, Friend/Helper
(Stourbridge, England)

Wendy remembers helping with house cleaning, especially all the windows, whilst Chris remembers helping Rob in the woods with logging. Evenings were spent cutting round stamps, enjoying deep conversation and much laughter. Visited 1981/1982.

Chris and Wendy Bull (née Smither), Helpers
(Dunstable/High Wycombe, England)

Introduced to The Mill by Isobel Vale, our first visit was in 1973 and Rob and Lil's warm welcome and their legendary hospitality encouraged us to return with family and church friends from England several times. We have prayed and supported Rob and Lil's ministry and been inspired by their love for and dedication to reaching children with the Gospel. Memories of The Mill include: playing Null and Pit; Semmel rolls; great fun; beautiful surroundings; iced coffee; walking on the Untersberg mountain; watching a royal wedding; Lil feeding us well and always keeping us on track; building an igloo in knee-deep snow; Rob's pancakes and popcorn; momentous Christmas meals together and a hot summer's day for a Koidl/Schunneman wedding!

Dave and Laraine Cook, Campers/Helpers/Friends
(Reading/Poole, England)

We arrived in Austria in 1964, with a six-month-old baby, leaving behind parents and twelve siblings thousands of miles away. God had a family in Austria waiting for us, and our favourite gathering place of all missionaries was The Mill. Nearly all our annual field conferences took place there, and it was home to all our children and poodle, Bonnie. Sadly, my wife and I ran over Bonnie whilst 'tubing[5]' and broke her leg. She survived and had four puppies[6], one of which was given to Rob and Lil.

Ralph and Verna Harvey, Missionaries/Friends
(New Jersey, USA)

Our memories are of Elizabeth and Georg's wedding at The Mill when members of our families, the Christophers and the

---

[5] 'Tubing' is the equivalent of tobogganing, Mill-style, using the inner tube of lorry or tractor tyres.

[6] The puppy's name was Asher (ginger colour) and a companion for Schufti, Rob's dog.

Keables, were present. Our grandchildren John and Hannah want to carry on that fellowship with their cousins.

**Peter and Brenda Christopher, Relatives
(Eltham, London)**

My parents often took us to The Mill to visit Bob and Lilian. In 1961 I was four, but can remember our drive down a very rough road, over a rickety wooden bridge to a basic building, bare concrete floors, no doors between rooms, but just blankets hanging in door frames. Always exciting to visit, lots going on and great opportunities to explore. Happy memories and more memorable visits in later years.

**Peter and Sandra Simpson, Son of Missionaries,
Barbara and Brian Simpson (Southampton, England)**

I was backpacking in Europe with some friends in 1978 and called The Mill from the train station in Salzburg, hoping to serve there, in exchange for a place to sleep and eat. Within a couple of weeks, The Mill became our home away from home. Such kindness and love. At that time, Bob was struggling with back pain, and as we helped, he let us know we were the answer to his prayers. He was so encouraging whatever we did. We saw an amazing commitment to the Lord, the Austrians and the ministry.

**Yvonne Miller, Helper/Friend
(Malvern, Pennsylvania, USA)**

My family lived in Austria for seven years when I was a child, and we spent a lot of time at the Schwaigmühle, sometimes at conferences but also personal visits. I have fond memories of

The Mill, Rob and Lil's friendship and hospitality, and their selfless service and love for the Lord.

Ron Del Mar, Son of Missionary Friends
(Kennewick, Washington State, USA)

I first visited the Schwaigmühle in 1968, having been given the Schunnemans' contact details from my church minister. Many visits followed. I helped muck out the sheep and pluck a goose as well as visits to the Yugoslav mission in Salzburg with Steve and Helen Torbico. Above all, there was The Mill hospitality afforded to all visitors whether on a planned visit, at a Christian conference or just popping in for a decent cup of tea on a walk from the Hotel Vötterl.

John Harrison, Helper and Friend
(Grove Park, London, England)

We worked in Vienna 1979–1983 and were planning a ski holiday for some of our contacts. The Schwaigmühle was recommended by our field director. We visited for our skiing weekend, and so began friendship with the Schunnemans and daughter, Elizabeth, and later her husband, Georg. We have maintained a friendship with them all. Our kids share with us very happy memories of the Schunneman family and the Schwaigmühle.

Devere and Lee Curtiss, then with Greater Europe
Mission, Austria
(Colorado Springs, USA)

As a young child, I remember the smell of freshly baked rolls for breakfast prepared by Lil in the kitchen. Her ham, egg and noodle dish is still the best I've ever had – I can still taste it in my head. Bob – always making, mending, digging or building – usually involving a cement mixer! He taught me some wood carving in the workshop above the garage. Above all, I remember the warmth of lovely evenings spent singing, studying the Bible and praying, which made such an impression on me. Such fun and laughter, a cherished part of my childhood.

Katie Setchell (née Muggeridge). My Parents, Len and Sylvia Muggeridge, and all our family visited in the 1970s. Helpers/Friends (Dunstable/Trowbridge)

My husband and I visited the Schwaigmühle in the early eighties, sent from our church in Birmingham. Dave was a gardener, and I helped inside. Our days started with prayer and Bible reading. Rob and Lil were so kind and hard-working. I still change duvet covers in the efficient way taught by Lil!

Margaret Jefferies, Helper (Cumbria, England)

I visited The Mill several times and always found a welcome there. Fellowship, not only in person to person but also in the work. In snowy conditions, I got onto the roof of The Mill in order to shovel snow and remember digging our way out of the drive after a 40/50cms overnight snowfall had blocked us in. I also learned how to ski and climbed the Untersberg with Rob on a clear summer's day.

Ernie Abbott, Cousin/Helper (UK/Singapore)

I visited The Mill frequently in the 1970s and 1980s, staying overnight when driving between Romania and the UK and then Slovenia and the UK. There were short holidays too. Visiting was always a sheer delight, thanks to Rob and Lil's unstinting hospitality, warm fellowship and friendship – the shared evening prayer times, the fun and laughter and the opportunity for outdoor jobs (chopping logs, building a woodpile, chopping maxi icicles off the roof); all gave me a welcome change from academic work. I watched Elizabeth grow up, and I remember the dogs, Schufti and Asher, who watched my every move, hoping to be taken on a long forest walk. Altogether, it was a wonderful home that radiated God's love and faithfulness.

Margaret Davis, Friend/Helper
(Medvode, Slovenia)

My first memory of The Mill was a trip with the Slavic Gospel Association, staying overnight, then later, another visit with a group of young people from Upton Vale Baptist Church, when we helped Rob with lifting buckets of wet concrete up to the top floor. Another memory was dealing with blocked sewer pipes late at night but by 2a.m. the problem was solved. Over the years, I had the privilege of spending a lot of time with Rob – we had different mission work, but were working for the same Lord. When Dot and I lived in Großgmain at the Rosenhof in the early 1980s, we were so grateful for those Saturday afternoon cups of tea and natter. Rachel and Mark still talk about Uncle Rob's swings.

Dot and Les Tidball, Workers and Friends/Missionaries
(Torquay, England)

I first met Lil and Rob in 1964, following a Christian Nurses Conference and was taken by a friend to meet 'a pair of missionaries'. That was when The Mill belonged to WMC. I watched the ministry grow. It was fun driving children to Kindergarten in a bus, along narrow lanes, on the wrong side of the road and sometimes in the snow, finding fresh ways of cooking mincemeat as well as cooking food for Schufti, the dog. I spent many happy holidays helping out at The Mill, with a stream of wonderful people who then used The Mill as a base before smuggling Bibles into Eastern Europe. A big adventure was when in freezing temperatures and for three travel days, I accompanied Lil and Rob, and baby Elizabeth back from England to The Mill. Our friendship has lasted all these years. Seeing how Lil and Rob made the centre work, sometimes under huge pressure, but by the grace of God, made a lasting impression on my life. I thank God for them.

Berry Rathgen [née Jackson], Helper/Friend
(Cowes, Victoria, Australia)

Appendix 3

List of Orphans

The ten children lived firstly in St. Jakob, near Salzburg, and then at the Schwaigmühle in Großgmain until 1964. Prior to this date, the Austrian authorities had given permission for the nine children to be adopted by Joe and Lee Coulson, and they all went to live in America (Fritz had died in 1961).

Eveline Marie Coulson-Okopide	b. 16.09.1952
Robert Coulson	b. 09.12.1952 d. 20.01.2021
Margarete Carmen Coulson-Dunlap	b. 21.11.1953
Geraldine Rose Coulson-Lott	b. 23.01.1953
(Gertrude at birth)	
Wilma Coulson	b. 24.02 1954
Josef Alfred Coulson	b. 08.04.1954
Peter Hladec-Coulson	b. 19.12.1954
Fritzi Hladec (Peter's twin)	b. 19.12.1954 d. 14.02.1961
Betty Anne Coulson (Eveline's half-sister)	b. 25.05.1955
Eduard Coulson	b. 02.07.1955 d. 22.12.1998

Appendix 4

Missionaries in an Austrian Context

What is a Missionary?

'The Mill in the Schwaig', focused on the work of the Schunnemans in a particular missional context in Austria and how they were supported by an organisation. Some other missionaries, doing different kinds of work, were also mentioned. So, is it possible then, to define the actual role of a 'missionary'? A simple answer is 'yes', for a Christian missionary is someone who wants to tell others about the Christian faith, and the term 'evangelism' is used to describe this activity. In one sense, all Christians are missionaries and evangelists, and they could fulfil this role in their home country. However, it would not be possible to be a full-time missionary at the same time as being fully employed in a job.

The term 'missionary' has come to mean someone who goes to another place/country and works on a specific project, maybe within a church setting or some other activity involving members of the community. Usually, this role will be full-time. The missionary will most likely have had some training prior to arrival and will be supported, both financially and in prayer, by a mission organisation, a church, or individuals back home.

Some missionaries feel a particular calling to certain countries, and some countries are more open to accepting missionaries than others. This book has highlighted Austria as a place of potential Christian mission, so what is it about Austria that has prompted missionaries to work there? A very brief look into the religious and political history of the country may shed some light on this matter.

Austria's Catholic Tradition: Past and Present

Christianity is the predominant religion in Austria with Catholicism being the strongest denomination. This is a historical situation, for after the Protestant Reformation spread across Europe, including Austria, this was followed by the Counter-Reformation in 1545. Following that time, Catholicism became the national and established church. A large number of Catholic churches can be seen across the country, and even in smaller towns and villages, there is likely to be a Catholic church. Some sources suggest that attendance at Catholic services is not as strong as in the past, except perhaps at festival times and rites of passage, for example, christenings, marriage and death ceremonies. For those members, by child baptism into the Catholic and Lutheran churches, there is an obligatory church tax.

Growth of Other Religions and Some Protestant Churches

Meanwhile, some other religious groups are growing. In recent years, the number of immigrants coming into Austria has increased, with Islam becoming stronger in its representation, particularly in the larger cities.

Protestants, that is non-Catholics, form a very small minority of the population. Within this group, there are some free churches experiencing a growth in membership. These churches would be termed 'evangelical' with a strong emphasis on preaching and teaching from the Bible. It's estimated that as large and growing as some of these Christian communities are, in total, they only represent about 0.4% of the population and are probably not much more than about thirty years old. Others go back, maybe sixty to seventy years. Some of these evangelical churches were started way back by American, Swiss or German missionaries. Most Austrians, whose roots are in the Catholic tradition, are unlikely to encounter such evangelical Christian groups or individuals unless they live in a large Austrian city. However, in recent times, more evangelical Christian churches are springing up in some of the smaller Austrian towns or cities.

Looking Back: The Political Situation Post-WWII

Austria's geographical and political history has been complicated for long periods of time. Put simply, over hundreds of years the country had been under the jurisdiction of other countries and lost some of its own lands. Following WWII, several European countries, including Austria, were re-establishing themselves and seeking to secure a national identity. For ten years, 1945–1955, the Allied Forces occupied four different areas of Austria:

i] Salzburg & Upper Austria – America; ii] Vorarlberg & North Tyrol – France; iii] East Tyrol, Carinthia & Styria – Britain; iv] Burgenland, Lower Austria & part of Upper Austria – Soviet Union. Vienna was also divided into four zones. The role of the Allied Forces was to support and build up the country. Austria did not become a totally independent country until 1955.

Missionary Support for Austria: Past and Present

From the eighteenth century onwards, it's probably true to say that some of the early free churches were the forerunners of the Evangelical Movement in Austria. However, due to war and other political factors, the Evangelical Movement had difficulty in truly establishing itself. Things became much more encouraging as WWII came to an end, with some shared missional work across borders.

There is evidence that some missionary organisations and individuals began to work in Austria post-WWII. In order to gain entry, missionaries had to demonstrate that their work contributed to the country. For example, the Slavic Gospel Association arrived around 1950, working with Displaced Persons of Eastern Europe, in some of the camps in Austria and beyond. The organisation was supporting on a social and practical level but was also providing spiritual support through literature and Christian activity. This way, Christian missionaries were 'accepted' into the country. This is just one example of missional support in Austria. With the Allied Forces in residence for ten years, the Austrian authorities were used to different countries and agencies supporting their country in many ways.

And so, to the present day. A quick Internet search reveals that there are missionary opportunities in Austria, some short term and some longer term. It's clear that individuals have to support themselves financially, or be supported from elsewhere, and usually these opportunities relate to the support of such groups as refugees or other needy groups. Some missionaries are involved in supporting church work, but the same funding mechanisms would also apply. In addition, anyone entering Austria would be required to possess the relevant legal documentation.

Within the Protestant tradition, and unlike some other countries, for example England and America, Austria does not have a long tradition of Christian revival and theological education. There are few Bible colleges and church training institutions. As a result, church ministers/pastors are rarely full-time, as such posts are not generally supported financially. Some Austrian pastors may be paid partially by their church, but would also have paid employment elsewhere, in order to be able to support themselves and their family. This situation does not encourage potential pastors to train for a church role through theological study, as they don't see full-time church work as a viable vocation alongside family life.

It wasn't until 2013 that the Federation of Evangelical Churches of Austria was officially recognised by the Government. Prior to this time, free churches had not been granted official church status. Today, missionaries supporting church work would be seeking to give good Bible teaching, help Christian leaders to develop their ministries and encourage congregations to reach their families and friends with the Christian message.

Appendix 5

A Taste of Austria: Some Favourite Recipes from The Mill (1964–1987) and Other Dishes

Gulasch

Definitely a favourite at The Mill, and very popular across Austria. Gulasch originated from Hungary, and as it became part of Austrian cuisine, different recipes have emerged. This one is the classic beef gulasch. It serves 6, and any leftovers keep well. 50 minutes to prepare and then about 3 hours of slow cooking.

Ingredients

1 kg onions, chopped
Oil
2 tablespoons tomato puree

3 tablespoons paprika powder (sweet)
2 tablespoons paprika powder (hot)
1 litre water
Salt and pepper
1 teaspoon ground caraway
1 tablespoon marjoram
1 kg beef, cut into chunks
A little flour and water for thickening (optional)

Method

1. Peel and chop onions finely. Fry until golden brown in a large saucepan with plenty of oil. Then stir in tomato puree, lower the heat, and add the paprika powders, stirring well.
2. Pour over a litre of warm water, adding salt and pepper and all the herbs listed above. Increase heat.
3. Bring to the boil and then simmer, uncovered for 30 mins, after which lower heat.
4. Season meat with salt and pepper and add to liquid (no need to fry meat first). Cover and cook on a low heat for about 3 hours. Check from time to time, stirring, and adding a little cold water if necessary.
5. The mixture should be thick enough but if not, thicken with a little flour and water.

In Austria, this would be served with Semmel bread rolls and dumplings, which could be substituted with boiled potatoes, pasta or noodles, and a green salad.

Guten Appetit!

Wiener Schnitzel/Breaded Veal Cutlets

Wiener Schnitzel is a very popular dish across Austria. Popular alternatives are pork, chicken or turkey schnitzel, which is made in the same way.

Serves 4.

Prep time about 20 mins then 20 mins of frying time.

Ingredients

4 cutlets/fillets of veal/pork/chicken/turkey
Plate/shallow dish of flour (approx. 4 tablespoons) mixed with a little salt and pepper
2 eggs beaten, in shallow dish
Plate/shallow dish of 4 oz/113 g fine breadcrumbs
Oil for frying
Lemon wedges to serve

Method

1. Prepare cutlets/fillets by rinsing, patting dry with a paper towel and cutting off excess fat. Pound cutlets/fillets on both sides with meat hammer/rolling pin to tenderise and flatten. (Only veal and pork fillets need to be pounded.)
2. Have each of the three dishes/bowls ready in order: flour, eggs, breadcrumbs.
3. Heat oil in large frying pan.
4. Take each cutlet/fillet individually, covering both sides with flour, then dip into the egg mixture and finally into breadcrumb mixture.

5. One after the other, place cutlets/fillets into a hot frying pan, medium heat and fry for 3–5 mins, turning occasionally. Ensure all cutlets/fillets are cooked well.
6. When cutlets/fillets are golden brown on both sides, remove from pan, and if desired, place on kitchen roll to absorb excess oil.
7. Cutlets/fillets can be kept warm in the oven until you are ready to serve the full meal.

Serve with boiled potatoes dressed with butter and parsley and a green salad, of lettuce and cucumber, dressed with oil and vinegar.

Guten Appetit!

Erdäpfelsalat/Potato Salad

This was definitely a favourite dish at The Mill. Very good with grilled Wiener sausages. Frankfurter sausages would be a suitable substitute. Austrians make potato salad without mayonnaise and sometimes with a warm dressing, but this recipe has a typical cold dressing.

Serves 4 and ready within 30 mins.

Ingredients

600 g potatoes (waxy sort is best)
60 g red onions, finely chopped
3 tablespoons apple vinegar
6 tablespoons oil
Salt and pepper
Pinch of sugar
Chives to decorate

Method

1. Boil potatoes with skin on, until soft but not mushy. Peel and slice while warm.
2. Peel and finely chop onions and season with vinegar, oil, salt and pepper.
3. Add a little sugar and taste.
4. Place potatoes in serving dish, pour over dressing and sprinkle with fresh chives.

Guten Appetit!

Käsespätzle/Cheese Spätzle

Everyone has heard of macaroni cheese and this was often made at The Mill. Cheese spätzle can perhaps be described as an Austrian version of mac cheese but maybe even better? Some recipes add nutmeg to the batter mix. Fried sliced bacon can also be added and placed between the layers of cooked spätzle. The onions are always cooked last and placed on top of the dish.

Serves 2–3.

Prep and cooking time 45 mins. Then 20 mins of oven cooking time.

Ingredients

2 eggs
½ cup of milk
½ teaspoon salt
½ teaspoon pepper
1 ½ cups of flour
1 tablespoon butter
1 onion sliced thinly
1 cup shredded Gruyere or Emmental cheese

Method

1. In a large bowl, combine eggs, milk, salt and pepper. Add flour, in stages. Stir with wooden spoon until smooth. Add a little more milk if batter is too thick. Rest batter for about 20 mins.
2. Meanwhile, fry bacon if using, and put to one side. Fry

onions in butter until golden. Put on one side.

3. Preheat oven to 350F/180C/Gas mark 4.

4. Over a large pan of simmering water, pour batter, in stages, through colander, potato ricer or spätzle maker. In less than a minute, the spätzle will float to the top and will be ready. Scoop out with strainer/sieve. Place in a warm, buttered casserole dish. Layer the spätzle with cheese (and chopped bacon if using) ensuring some cheese is left to cover the top of the dish.

5. Finally, place the fried onions on top of the dish and cook in the oven for 15–20 mins until golden brown.

6. Serve with a green salad.

Guten Appetit!

Kaiserschmarrn/Emperor's Pancake

This sweet dish is named after the Austrian Emperor, Kaiser Franz Joseph I who, it seemed, was fond of sweet treats. It can be served on its own, though often Austrians enjoy it with a small portion of plum compote. Any soft fresh fruit or compote would go well with the pancake. This recipe provides 3–4 portions.

This is an Austrian-style pancake, so the texture may be a little different from what you know.

Ingredients

125 g plain flour
Salt
250 ml milk
4 large eggs separated
50 g butter
30 g icing sugar
Icing sugar for dusting

Method

1. In large bowl, mix flour and salt. Add milk, whisking until smooth. Add one egg yolk at a time, whisking well between each addition.
2. In another large bowl, whisk egg whites until very stiff. Then fold carefully into the batter mix.
3. Heat a non-stick frying pan, and add a good knob of butter. Once bubbling, add about a third of the batter

mixture and turn down the heat. Cover the pan with a lid for approximately 1–2 mins. When the base of the pancake is a golden colour, attempt a flip and add a little more butter. Cover with the lid again, until the underside is golden.

4. Sieve a little icing sugar over this first pancake and with spoons/spatula, roughly tear the pancake into bite-sized pieces. Then stir, so all the pieces look golden. Keep warm on a serving plate.

5. Repeat the process above, until all the batter mixture is used up.

6. Serve Kaiserschmarrn warm, dusted with plenty of icing sugar.

Guten Appetit!

Banana Topfen Crème Dessert

This was a favourite of campers at The Mill. It's an easy dessert to make, and if any ingredients are not available, they can be replaced with something similar. Topfen is an Austrian farmers' cheese and the best alternative is quark. Cream cheese or mascarpone also works well.

Serves 4.

Prep time 10 mins.

Ingredients

3 bananas

5 tablespoons lemon juice (preferably fresh)

2 tablespoons castor sugar (fine sugar)

1 packet vanilla sugar (or 1 teaspoon of vanilla extract)

500 g topfen/quark/mascarpone

Method

1. In a bowl, slice and mash bananas, adding the lemon juice (or bananas could be left in slices).
2. In another bowl, mix quark (or alternative) with castor sugar and vanilla sugar.
3. Add banana mixture to quark mixture and mix thoroughly. Add a drop of milk if consistency is too thick. Taste to check.
4. Spoon mixture into glass bowls and decorate with walnuts/chocolate flake.

Guten Appetit!

Appendix 6

Current Details of the Schwaigmühle

Freizeithaus Schwaigmühle runs as a self-catering camp and conference centre. It is situated in a quiet, beautiful location, in the middle of the Untersberg Nature Park. There are many hiking trails near and far, as well as a cable car up to the top of the mountain.

The nearest village is Großgmain, approximately ten minutes' drive away, or a sixty-minute walk. Castle ruins, a church, restaurants, a few shops and hotels make this a delightful small centre.

Salzburg is a twenty-minute drive away, and there is a limited bus service from Großgmain to Salzburg.

Freizeithaus Schwaigmühle, Latschenstrasse 12, 5084 Großgmain, Salzburg, Austria

https://schwaigmuehle.freizeiten.at/

The Mill, from a photograph by John Christopher

Looking across the road to Großmain church

Großmain castle ruins